Finding Stability
in
Times of Change

Richard Frost

Endulini Publishing

First published in 2022 by Endulini Publishing
Endulini House, Raleigh Road
Mowbray, Cape Town
Western Cape
South Africa 7700

ISBN 978-0-6397-3023-3
e-ISBN 978-0-6397-3024-0

This is a timely and helpful book. It is about change. Life is full of it of course. But while some change is welcome, energising and life giving, there is change that arrives like a storm or earthquake, uprooting even the most deeply rooted things in us. It leaves us destabilised. Off balance. For many, quite a lot of life feels like that right now.

Richard Frost's book explores how to find a place to stand in such times. The task needs wisdom and it takes practice. The book approaches this in a variety of ways. There are reflections from the Christian scriptures and the lives of people found there. There are resources drawn from Christian practices of prayer and spirituality. But also here are the stories of a variety of people who have journeyed through the most unsettling life changes. Their voices are honest and vulnerable and they earth this discussion in the toughest realities of life and faith. So the book feels like a conversation in the midst of the winds and the storms - with ourselves, with each other, with scripture and the hard won resources of Christian faith – and with God.

David Runcorn, writer, speaker, spiritual director & 'free range' priest

I read this book at a period in my own life when I was experiencing a great deal of change, from the relatively minor (returning by train from a much-needed holiday) to the more significant (major changes in my workplace). Richard Frost leads us gently through a process of identifying, understanding and responding to change. He weaves wisdom from the Christian tradition together with secular understandings of the treatment of stress. His book is perceptive and wise – a valuable guide on life's journey.

Morwenna Ludlow, historian, theologian and Anglican priest

At a time when the rate of change – of all kinds – far outstrips our ability to negotiate the transitions, Richard's book is undoubtedly timely. Whilst it is easy simply to encourage a believer in God to 'have faith', so often that is the one thing that may prove difficult in times of storm and stress. Richard draws on his experience of the Benedictine Rule with its emphasis on listening, conversion of life and stability, as well as the accounts of Jesus calming the storm on Lake Galilee to aid our search for wisdom. Many people find it easier to learn from stories than from theory, however wise and Biblical: and Richard uses these to good effect, looking at both Biblical characters, contemporary testimony and Jesus himself.

Given that those who are perhaps most in need of finding stability will by definition be facing challenging times, this book is neither too long nor too difficult a read. Several other authors are quoted and referenced for those who may want to dig deeper, but Richard's 'prescription' here should prove both accessible and reassuring for many.

Sheila Walker, priest & author

Read more endorsements at www.richardfrostauthor.com

Contents

Foreword

As I write these few words to introduce Richard Frost's latest book I have done something momentous. I have just written to my bishop offering my resignation, announcing my retirement. It is a year away but I wanted to give him the time and space to appoint my successor. I have been at Southwark Cathedral since 1999. I came as that huge and in some ways feared moment of change was approaching: the Millennium. We had been warned that the change might mean that a bug would stop everything working, that life would fall off a cliff, that clocks and computers would stop. Midnight passed and life went on.

Richard quotes the Prime Minister, Boris Johnson, addressing the nation from Downing Street in March 2020, telling us that there was another bug, not a millennium one this time, but one that would bring life to a standstill, which would turn out to be a huge catalyst for change, which would become one of those lines of sand in our history that would require us to work out in future whether we are talking pre- or post-pandemic.

Change does produce feelings of both excitement and fear, it can create huge anxiety and Richard recognises this. When I retire, I will have been in stipendiary ministry for forty years, I will have been at the Cathedral for twenty-four of those years. My life has been formed, more by chance than decision, by the Benedictine principle of stabilitas. Of course, there has been massive change along the way. Those forty years, those twenty-four years, my lifetime so far, have seen constant, and at times overwhelming, change. But a great deal has stayed the same.

The storm on the sea which Richard uses as the story to hold what he offers to us is one of those critical moments in the gospels. When I am with pilgrims on the Sea of Galilee when the engines of the boat we are on are switched off, when someone gets up to read one of the accounts of the raging waters that seem to threaten the boat and the lives of all in it, when we then sing, as so many pilgrims do, the hymn 'Dear Lord and Father of mankind' you sense that we have all been in the same boat, in that storm-tossed boat. Some of the words of that hymn spoke to me on that occasion and speak to me now.

Take from our souls the strain and stress,
And let our ordered lives confess
The beauty of thy peace.

John Whitter, the author of that hymn, an American, living through the turbulent times of the nineteenth century, an abolitionist, caught up in the Civil War, knew that strain and stress for himself. He suffered a mental breakdown at one point but continued working when and as he could. He wrote out of his own experience in a nation that was facing the trauma of change, of embracing justice where injustice was dehumanising people around him.

We need strategies and tools for coping with change, coping with instability, and coping with the 'not knowing' that fills many of us with anxiety. This book contains lots that can help us on the way. It doesn't begin to suggest that change will go away, change is part of life, but we can be better prepared for it and ready to face it with the strength that comes through faith.

I don't know what my future will hold, nor do you. All I am able to do, all you are able to do, is step into the future, doing as Minnie Louise Haskins suggests in her popular poem, so beloved by The Queen and her father, known by us as 'The Gate of the Year' but called by the author 'God Knows'.

Go out into the darkness and put your hand into the Hand of God. That shall be to you better than light and safer than a known way.

**The Very Revd Andrew Nunn, Dean of Southwark,
London, July 2022**

1. Facing the strange

'Ch-ch-ch-ch-changes, Turn and face the strange.'

Change is nothing new, ever-present, and often faster than many of us find comfortable. Whether of our own choice or not, change is often accompanied by some unsettling companions such as waiting and uncertainty. Added to which we can also find ourselves dealing with the transition from one set of circumstances to another. Change, even when it's exciting and energising, can be unsettling and affect our sense of inner stability. As David Bowie's song 'Changes' says, we find ourselves having to 'Turn and face the strange.'[i]

Whether it's at work, home, church, or elsewhere, we can often feel resistant to change. Keeping things the same helps us feel safe – especially in a world that changes so much. In times of change, we're often keen to hold on to that which remains the same. We need stability. When something threatens our stability, such as change or uncertainty, as experienced by so many of us during the Coronavirus pandemic, for example, life feels unstable, life feels strange.

You may like to think about how your life has changed in the last 5, 10, 20 years, and how it might change in the next 5, 10, 20. Perhaps you are facing change at this precise moment?

Many people find change difficult.

It may be a relatively minor one to routine or the process by which a particular task is done – or even just getting a new smartphone! Larger scale changes can also be hard – whether it's a change of manager or minister; a change in family life at home; or in health due to accident or diagnosis - and also, sometimes, the adjustments involved when recovering from an illness.

At the core of why we find change difficult is partly down to the fact that while many aspects of the world around us can change quickly, we as human beings tend to change much more slowly.

It's rather like a pair of cog wheels that can't interlock properly – one is going at a different speed than the other. This 'mismatch' is often due to the fact that the core characteristics of who we are as individuals can take years to develop. It takes time to change.

The space between

Change often happens when something starts or stops – or one thing stops and another starts in its place. One job ends and another begins – or doesn't. Or we move from one home to another. Whether change takes place overnight or over a longer period, it can be the transition that takes time.

Transition is the internal adjustment to change and is intimately connected with the sense of who we are and where we belong during times of change.[ii] We may be able to plan and organise the practical aspects of change but managing the process of transition is often more difficult.

Even with the most positive and exciting changes – such as the birth of a child, getting married, beginning a new job, or becoming a Christian – it is common for people to experience periods of depression, stress, feelings of loss for what they have moved on from, or to have relationship problems in the processing of such change and transition. As someone put it, 'The ending and the beginning again are reminiscent of dying and re-birth. In a new situation, we are different. Our points of reference have changed.'[iii]

Mark Bradford wrote 'As much as we may wish for seasons of certainty, in which the ground beneath our feet is firm and unmoving, the truth is that such times are surprisingly rare. More often than not, we find ourselves living through seasons of transition, disruption, even crisis. In these times, an old reality has come to an end, yet a new pattern has not yet presented itself and we find ourselves living in the void in the middle.'[iv] Mark Bradford describes this void as 'the space between' and argues that we can spend a lot of our lives living in such spaces: and they are not always the most comfortable.

In times of change, and for that matter in times when change isn't taking place, it is natural to worry about what it is we are waiting for or waiting to happen or not happen, and to worry about the possible consequences. The 'What ifs'...

We might still recognise God's presence in such times and trust God in them – but such is the nature of waiting and transition that our anxieties mean we can easily lose sight of the one who loves us more than we can ever imagine.

Such anxieties are not signs of failure or that our faith or trust are lacking. God understands our feelings and our difficulties. These times of transition, waiting and uncertainty are all part of human experience and it's natural to want to run away from them at times. We find it hard to face the strange.

The times they are a-changin'

In many ways, Bob Dylan's famous song sums up the last few decades and my guess is he may not have anticipated just how much the times would change since he wrote it way back in 1963.[v]

We live in a world where there have been massive changes in those last sixty years not least global economic and political change and the awareness of climate change. And then in much more recent times, there was the Coronavirus pandemic – what a lot of change that brought about. Add to that, times of global uncertainty brought about by events such as Russia's invasion of Ukraine and in Europe, the increased price of energy and the cost of living crisis. And then the death of Queen Elizabeth II – such a figure of stability in a changing world.

The way we communicate has changed with social media, e-mail, the internet, and smartphones often replacing talking face to face. We can watch our favourite TV programmes and follow breaking news at times and on devices to completely suit ourselves.

There have been changes in families and relationships such as the increased number of blended families. Changes in social mobility and adult children still at or returning to live at home often for economic or other reasons. Changes in the nature of marriage, same-sex partnerships and cohabitation. The world is also a very different place in relation to attitudes towards gender, identity and sexuality. There's been a massive growth of virtual (internet) relationships and people who have no offline (in other words, no face-to-face) friends.

For many, gone is the job for life, 9-5, Monday-Friday working pattern. Many workplaces have a long-hours culture and are target-driven, unstable, highly pressured environments. An increasing number of people do most of their work at home (not just because of the pandemic – that workplace change was happening before all that), bringing with it not just freedom but also isolation from colleagues. For many, the 24/7 culture has displaced the value that Sundays used to have.

There have been major medical advances and improved awareness of mental ill health in particular. People are living longer and that has brought not only increased care demands but also higher levels of activity in older people and positive changes in attitudes towards retirement and death. And, of course, what we all understood as 'normal life' changed dramatically and disturbingly as a result of the pandemic.

Churches are changing – at last, you might say! During the pandemic lockdowns, the arrival of online services reached out to so many and Google searches for 'prayer' were at a height. Alongside struggling churches, particularly in rural areas, there has been the growth of church plants and fresh expressions, such as Messy Church, within which we see the church engaging with people where they are – although the (sometimes unrealistic) desire for them to 'come to church' remains as strong as ever. Alongside that, we live in a multi-faith community and differing interpretations of the word 'spirituality'.

Whether it's a change of place (although having moved 22 times in my life, it does get a bit wearing); a change of job status (I moved on from paid employment in 2018 – I thoroughly enjoyed my job but am also enjoying this next stage of life); or a change in being the person we are (something I've actively cultivated at several points), change is a constant factor in the lives of many people. Some changes may not affect you personally – but others may be at the forefront of your mind at this very moment.

Stormy weather

This book aims to explore how change affects us and the different ways in which we can find stability in such times: stability based on the unchanging nature of God.

The Bible contains hundreds of examples of change. From being a baby in the bulrushes to a murderer to a leader of people, Moses experienced change. We can think of Sarah and Abraham having a child at their great age – life was certainly never the same again there. David was transformed from a humble shepherd to a powerful and somewhat flawed king.

While the lives of the disciples were changed beyond recognition when Jesus called them to follow him, in other ways their lives remained the same. Some were called from the daily rhythms of fishing in Lake Galilee to an extraordinary experience of being with Jesus. Yet their work and home life also continued and we can see the impact of that change upon them. For example, the brothers James and John were still working for their father, Zebedee, a well-to-do businessman. Is their, at times, impetuous behaviour and outlandish requests to sit in heaven at the Lord's side symptomatic of the difficulty of their time of transition? After all, we can all be more irritable and irrational in times of change...

Throughout this book, we will consider examples from the Bible, especially from Jesus' own life and experience. In particular, we're going to reflect on how the event of Jesus calming the storm on Lake Galilee can help us. First, we'll consider how the storm itself symbolises times of change, transition and uncertainty. Secondly, we'll think about the impact it had on the disciples and how that reflects our own reaction to 'stormy weather'. And finally, we'll look at how the calming influence of Christ helps us to find stability – and some very practical ways you might like to consider in your own life.

Three of the four gospels record this particular event and each account is fairly similar. That may be because Mark (4:35-41) wrote his account first and the writers of both Matthew's (8:23-27) and Luke's (8:22-25) Gospels may well have drawn on his writing as well as other sources. This event is one of nine 'nature miracles' by Jesus. Jesus performed miracles in response to people's faith; to back up his teaching about the coming of the Kingdom of God through him and his works; out of compassion for others; and, as was the case on this occasion, to instill faith in him where none or little was present.[vi] The miracle forced the disciples to ask themselves, and each other, 'Who then is this?' (Mark 4:41a). That is a question we will also ask.

Also included is wisdom from other writers and personal contributions from a number of ordinary, everyday people who tell their own stories of finding stability in times of change (or not).

We will also think about the value of day to day activities alongside paying intentional attention to God to help find that sometimes elusive thing called stability.

One of the threads running through this book is drawn from Benedictine spirituality. I'm a lay member of a Benedictine monastic community (an Oblate) so that approach influences some aspects of how I encounter Christ in today's ever-changing world. You may like to read Life with St Benedict which offers daily reflections on the Rule of St Benedict and how it relates to 21st Century living.[vii]

The Benedictine monastic tradition is based on three approaches – listening to God, conversion of life (or change) and stability. We live in a world where change is often feared, stability can be elusive and busyness interferes with listening to God. As we listen to God, we become increasingly aware that in order to change, stability is needed; and in order to be stable, we are also to change.[viii]

Before moving on to the next chapter, you may like to take some time to think about:

- Which changes in your life have you handled well?

- What did you learn from those times of change?

- Are you one who 'turns to face the strange' – or keeps facing in the same direction?

- It may be that you're experiencing change, transition, uncertainty or waiting at the moment. What do you need to do to help manage all that is bringing about?

2. There's a storm coming

'From this evening I must give the British people a very simple instruction. You must stay at home.'[ix]

You may remember that announcement of the first pandemic lockdown by the then British Prime Minister, Boris Johnson on 23 March 2020. There had been some warning signs in the previous few weeks, hadn't there? A tentative 'weather forecast' you might say, but not many quite anticipated the sheer impact of the storm. Suddenly, everything changed.

As we will see, for the disciples sailing across Lake Galilee a storm blew up quickly and its impact was immediate. The 'storms of life' can be like this for us. For example, it's common to hear about someone involved in an accident or other traumatic event receiving 'life-changing injuries'. We hear about people arriving at work to be told their jobs have been made redundant and sent home the very same day. Life is going along quite smoothly and then... a storm happens. Suddenly, everything changed.

Some changes can be more gradual – and by no means is all change negative. Seeing children grow up and mature or someone flourishing in their career or somebody recovering from depression, for example, can be very positive times of change. You may like to think about positive changes that have taken place in your own life and those around you.

All the same, some gradual changes take place without us realising it and there are those occasions when other people notice changes in us before we do. For example, the awareness that we're not able to do some of the things we used to do as we get older or the gradual deterioration of a marriage or a working relationship between colleagues.

Storm force

As well as the speed at which the change occurs, another significant factor is the strength of the storm.

If you're a sailor or a follower of the Shipping Forecast then you'll be familiar with the Beaufort Scale – or the Beaufort Wind Force Scale to give it its full name. Developed in 1806 by the Irishman, Francis Beaufort, a Royal Navy officer and later Rear Admiral, it's been revised and updated over the years but still forms the basis of marine forecasts, a practical measure for describing the intensity of the wind based on how it affects the sea.[x]

You may have also come across another scale which considers the effects of the 'stormy' aspects of life upon the boat we sail in. In 1967, psychiatrists Thomas Holmes and Richard Rahe studied how stressful life events contribute to illness. They surveyed more than 5,000 people and asked them to say whether they had experienced any of a series of 43 life events in the previous two years. Each event, called a 'Life Change Unit', had a different numerical 'weight' for the stress it caused. For example, a change in church circumstances was 'weighted' at 19; retirement at 45; the death of a spouse at 100 etc. The more events the patient added up in the two-year period, the higher the score. The higher the score, the more likely the person was to become ill.[xi] This approach also recognises the cumulative stress which occurs when we experience a number of difficult life events in a relatively short period of time. Importantly, it can help us think about what we may or may not take on or experience in the future and how best to help ourselves stay well as a result.

Ok. So, I've used the S-word.

Stress.

Yes, the word 'stress' can be used too lightly but there are times when the pressures we all face, both in work and outside of work, outweigh our ability to cope with them. There is no such thing as 'good stress'. We all need a degree of pressure to function well but harmful levels of stress can lead to physical, emotional, and behavioural issues – such as heart problems, muscular pain, skin complaints or being more irritable, or having sleep difficulties. Left unaddressed, stress-related issues can also develop in to mental health conditions such as anxiety or depression.

Our ability to cope with the 'storms' we face in life is key to our experience of stress and the impact such events have upon us. For example, starting a new job might be an exciting experience if everything else in our life is stable and positive. But if one starts a new job when we've just moved into a new house, or our partner is ill, or we're experiencing money problems, we might find it hard to cope.[xii]

Now, and I must emphasise this is in a purely non-scientific way, if we were to combine the Beaufort Scale with insights from the work of Holmes and Rahe (The Social Readjustment Rating Scale [SRSS], to give it its proper name) we can begin to understand the nature of life's storms a bit more. Doing this may also help us understand both the impact of such events and how best to face them.

First, though, a couple of notes about the table that follows. The terms used for life events are taken from the Holmes-Rahe scale and shown in exactly the same order that they used – but it's your author who has put them into 'storm categories' based on The Beaufort Scale.

Secondly, different life events affect people in different ways so, for example, some may feel that a change in sleeping habits causes a rough sea not just a slight to moderate one. People from different cultural backgrounds may also feel differently about the potential impact of particular life events.

Thirdly, it's also worth noting that having been developed over 50 years ago, the Holmes-Rahe Scale doesn't take into account changes in society since then. You may like to think about where you would put events such as domestic violence; racial discrimination; sexual abuse; change in sexual or gender identity; being single; loneliness;

the impact of social media and computers. There'll be others too –
and, of course, the pandemic raised many events into a higher
category all by itself. And also have a think about what you would
write in the empty boxes – what makes you feel calm or causes only
slight ripples?

Scale	Strength	The Effect	Life events
12	Hurricane	Phenomenal	Death of a spouse
11	Violent storm	Very High	Divorce; Marital separation; Imprisonment; Death of a close family member
10	Storm	Very High	Personal injury or illness; Marriage
9	Strong gale	High	Dismissal from work; Marital reconciliation; Retirement; Change in the health of family member
8	Gale	Very rough to High	Pregnancy; Sexual difficulties; Gain a new family member; Business readjustment; Change in financial state; Major mortgage
7	Near gale	Rough to Very rough	Death of a close friend; Change to a different line of work; Change in the frequency of arguments; Foreclosure of mortgage or loan

6	Strong breeze	Rough	Change in responsibilities at work; Child leaving home; Trouble with in-laws; Outstanding personal achievement; Spouse starts or stops work; Beginning or end of school; Change in living conditions
5	Fresh breeze	Moderate	Revision of personal habits; Trouble with a boss; Change in working hours or conditions; Change in residence; Change in schools
4	Moderate breeze	Slight to Moderate	Change in recreation; Change in church activities; Change in social activities; Minor mortgage or loan; Change in sleeping habits; Change in number of family reunions; Change in eating habits; Vacation; Major holiday; Minor violation of law
3	Gentle breeze	Slight	
2	Light breeze	Smooth (wavelets)	
1	Light air	Calm (rippled)	
0	Calm	Calm (glassy)	

So, to recap, changes can happen quickly or slowly and they can vary in strength or severity and also in their impact. And it's important not to underestimate the cumulative effect of a number of difficult life events.

As Mark Bradford put it, 'Beyond the storm, we may need to inspect any damage to the boat that is our lives and to consider what debris we are able to salvage. However, there will be new opportunities to sail again upon the waters and even expand our horizons.'[xiii]

We've considered some examples and it's important to remember that each of us will not only have different experiences but we will each respond in different and individual ways. The same event may affect a number of people but we won't necessarily respond in the same way that others do. Just because we cope with a particular thing happening doesn't mean to say another person will – and vice-versa.

Avoiding the storm

On that memorable day on Lake Galilee, despite all their experience and knowledge, the disciples had no choice. They couldn't escape the storm. They had to face up to it and cope with the impact.

But for many of us, instead of trying to cope with the storms, the times of change, it is very tempting to try to avoid them. It's even been called escapist or avoidance coping. 'Instead of dealing with the impact and the stress by being proactive and seeking solutions, we think and act in ways all geared to deny, minimise, or avoid what is stressing us,' wrote Sheri Jacobson.[xiv]

As another writer put it, 'You take deliberate actions to avoid the difficulties of the change. For instance, you might deliberately miss training for a new working process, or show up too late to attend a meeting.'[xv] We may want to pretend that it's not happening: to bury our head in the sand. The only thing that happens when we bury our head in the sand is we can't breathe. We end up being suffocated by the impact of the change and don't learn how to deal with other storms that affect us.

Writing about escapist coping, Jeremy Sherman provides this salutary challenge to those of us who hold Christian belief:

> 'The most escapist coping strategies tend to come bundled with optimistic, absolute-faith philosophies, religious, spiritual, political or otherwise. Faith is coping by hoping, embracing an optimistic belief that things will work out the way that your philosophy predicts they will. These reduce stress by narrowing your perspective, coping by hoping, and as a result, by noping, saying "Nope, I won't look at that. Nope, I don't have to listen to you. Nope, I'll cling to my faith and ignore everything that counters it."... Shunning the unpleasant is a dangerous way to live. Shunning it proudly because you have faith that you already know it all is especially dangerous.'[xvi]

Acknowledging that all of us are escapists to a degree, Sherman continues by saying 'You'll be happier (and healthier company for others) in the long run if you choose strategies that free and even encourage you to face what's true.'

'Many people spend a great deal of time and energy trying to avoid change, but it will inevitably catch up to them,' wrote Kathleen Smith. 'If you can learn to cope with change, you'll lower your risk for anxiety and depression. Your relationships will flourish, and your body will feel healthier. But if you can't cope with change, only a minor amount of stress can make you feel overwhelmed by life. You might also struggle to set and meet the goals you have for yourself.'[xvii]

Thomas Merton summed up the avoidance approach very succinctly: 'Indeed, the truth that many people never understand until it is too late, is that the more you try to avoid suffering, the more you suffer because smaller and more insignificant things begin to torture you.'[xviii]

So, armed with an awareness of the nature of change and the effects of storms, let's get ready to make the journey across the lake with some reassuring words from Julian of Norwich: '(Jesus) said not: "Thou shalt not be tempest-tossed; thou shalt not be work-weary; thou shalt not be distressed." But he did say: "Thou shalt not be overcome."'[xix]

We are to turn and face the strange.

3. Setting sail

We begin our journey by sitting on the shore.

Maybe it's a journey we've thought about for some time. A journey to the next stage of life. A new job. A new relationship. Whether or not to move home. To have children. To get married or remain single. Retirement. To change churches.

We may have looked at the metaphorical weather forecast: thinking about the pros and cons of the journey. Where might the rough waters be? What would provide shelter? We might have talked to others to gain their support and advice and allowed ourselves to be challenged too.

And what's in our suitcase? Are there things we need to leave behind on this journey – the hurts, the memories, the things we'll miss? What do we need to take with us? And where's the life jacket?

We may have felt a sense of calling for this journey. After all, Jesus said: 'Let us go across to the other side of the lake.' If we are honest before God and not trying to deceive ourselves, that in itself can be confusing. Is it Jesus calling us into the boat or is it me deciding that

I am the best person to accompany him... God's will or my will, our confusion cries.

But it's hard, isn't it? Hard doing or not doing something when others expect us to because deep down inside we know God is saying something different. It's hard doing what God wants us to do and listening to him when all that is going on around us is tough or changing. It's hard discerning what journey Jesus wants us to take – even when it's him who's asking us to get in the boat.

So we've done all we can to discern God's will (the best sailing conditions). We've prayed, we've talked, we've planned. We set sail...

And then... it happens.

There's a storm.

That new colleague who seemed so pleasant at the interview turns out to be a bully. The relationship which turns sour through coercion or domestic violence. The new home with dry rot or flammable cladding. The children... well that could be anything, really. The marriage which doesn't live up to expectations in the talking or the loving. The single life and its pressures from others to find 'the one'. A deterioration in health as retirement proceeds. The church and all its inevitable human failings.

Did I really get it so wrong?

Why did you allow me to enter such a situation, God?

Well, it was just like that for the disciples too.

Swamped

It had been a good day.

'Such a very large crowd gathered around him that he got into a boat on the lake and sat there, while the whole crowd was beside the lake on the land.' (Mark 4:1)

Always at pains to help his closest followers understand the meaning of his ministry, after teaching parables to the crowd, Jesus took time with the disciples on their own. 'With many such parables he spoke the word to them, as they were able to hear it; he did not speak to them except in parables, but he explained everything in private to his disciples.' (Mark 4:33-34)

No doubt the disciples listened to the teachings of Jesus along with the rest of the crowd but the event that was to follow shows they hadn't yet fully grasped the true nature of who Jesus was. John Drane observed, 'The purpose of miracles can be helpfully compared with the purpose of parables. To those who are willing to trust God, they are a vehicle of revelation. But to those whose minds are closed not even a miracle will bring the possibility of enlightenment.'[xx]

Evening came and it was time to leave the crowd and set off across the lake. One can imagine the disciples talking about all they had seen and heard that day. Asking each other about the parables and talking about who Jesus was. It had been a day to remember – not for the first time and not for the last. How they must have been both excited and content to set off in the boat on their journey of about eight miles. A couple of hours to share some food, watch the sunset, listen to the birds singing as dusk falls, one could almost say it was heavenly.

The world of the disciples has been changed through the presence of this man Jesus.

They set off. Something they have done hundreds of times before. There are others with them in other boats too. 'These men in the boat were very experienced fishermen,' Martin Turner observed, 'they had never done anything else, they knew the lake and all its foibles. They would not have gone out onto the lake if they had thought there was any danger at all, especially if Jesus was with them, the teacher they valued and loved so much. So there seemed to be no risk or they would not have set out.'[xxi]

It's a familiar routine. It's comfortable – so much so, that Jesus falls asleep.

> 36 And leaving the crowd behind, they took him with them in the boat, just as he was. Other boats were with him. 37 A great gale arose, and the waves beat into the boat, so that the boat was already being swamped. 38 But he was in the stern, asleep on the cushion; and they woke him up and said to him, 'Teacher, do you not care that we are perishing?' 39 He woke up and rebuked the wind, and said to the sea, 'Peace! Be still!' Then the wind ceased, and there was a dead calm. 40 He said to them, 'Why are you afraid? Have you still no faith?' 41 And they were filled with

great awe and said to one another, 'Who then is this, that even the wind and the sea obey him?' (Mark 4:36-41)

Set in the hills of northern Israel, the Sea of Galilee is nearly 700 feet below sea level. The sea's location makes it subject to sudden and violent storms as the wind comes over the eastern mountains and drops suddenly onto the sea. Storms are especially likely when an east wind blows cool air over the warm air that covers the sea. The cold air (being heavier) drops as the warm air rises. This sudden change can produce furious storms in a short time.[xxii] Sailing towards the western shore, the disciples were caught unawares. Unprepared for the onslaught that caused the boat to be swamped.

It is a common and somewhat frustrating aspect of life that things can be going along quite normally and then something difficult happens. Maybe we've had a particularly good day with other people – or a lovely time without them. Or we're pleased with something we've achieved or bought or received. We've had a special blessing or uplifting time of worship or just feeling very close to God. We want it to last forever... and it doesn't.

And it needn't even be a full-blown storm that rocks the boat. Just something that takes the edge off things. A misjudged word. An unwelcome text message. Or just plain and (at times not so) simple tiredness. It's often at those points when the Devil makes mischief too. When we're happy and content we can be an easy target.

It's the contrast that's often the killer, isn't it? We move from calm waters to being swamped more quickly than if it was the other way around – and it takes time to find stability again.

One wonders if there is also another very human attribute at play here. Other dynamics and thoughts come into play. It seems this is one of those occasions when we are perfectly capable of doing something but the fact someone else is there (for the disciples, Jesus) means we somehow drop one mark on the competency scale. There's an increased pressure to get it right which paradoxically results in not being able to do it as well as usual.

Yet, as Efrain Agosto observes, 'Not even the very experienced fishermen could do anything about (the storm). They turn to Jesus, presumably because of the powers that he has shown in healing sick people and exorcising demons. Maybe he can help them in this situation.' Agosto wonders if the fact Jesus is asleep, 'Negatively impacts the faith of the disciples, or perhaps their faith is not as strong as that of Jesus, who can sleep through this great storm, a sign of his faith in the face of calamity.'[xxiii]

'The story,' writes Mark Edington, 'is notable for the contrast between the quiet confidence of Jesus and the agonized worry of the disciples. He lies asleep, undisturbed by the tumult, while the disciples respond to the energy of the storm by expending energy of their own, vainly imagining human exertion can prove the equal of nature.'[xxiv]

Tossed about

Imagine yourself there for a moment. Maybe think about being one of the disciples in the boat. Or if it's easier, think of a parallel situation – perhaps having a meal with family or friends, for example.

Things start off well. It's companionable. Safe. Enjoyable.

Then something happens. A storm blows up. An argument breaks out.

Remember, when you have a group of people encountering exactly the same situation, everyone's reaction will be different. Some may be like Corporal Jones from Dad's Army – 'Don't panic, don't panic!' Others may make an excuse to leave. Some may give the impression of sitting serenely as if it wasn't affecting them at all. Some will be frightened or anxious.

How might you react?

In such heightened atmospheres, it's quite possible that voices will be raised. Things will be said in the heat of the moment that are unhelpful or hurtful. For the disciples, the noise of the storm would have been exceptionally loud so it's no wonder they shout at Jesus. Who knows, they may have been trying to control the boat for a while without disturbing him. This is a special passenger remember. He needs to rest. They may have tried to wake him to warn him of the danger. But with increasing panic and the noise of the storm, one of them ends up saying something in the heat of the moment: 'Do you not care that we are perishing?' And even that is potentially a sanitised version. But you can feel the desperation and the fear. 'Come on, we've been trying to control this boat, we need everyone to help not just lie there asleep!'

The disciples are afraid. And that fear is very real.

They will have heard of others lost in the storms of Lake Galilee. Mark's Gospel tells us there were other boats on this occasion too. Perhaps full of fishermen or people from the crowd wanting to follow Jesus like a group of admiring fans. Their boats are tossed about. They too are in danger. There is plenty to be scared about.

'The storms of life sometimes seem to come from nowhere. On occasion they can be of our own making,' writes Mark Bradford.[xxv] No doubt some of the disciples or those in other boats will have been blaming themselves (or others) for setting off. We all want to try and find reasons for when bad things happen. We might also interpret such times as God's punishment for something we've done or not done or bemoan the fact that 'Life is such a mess. Everything's going wrong and it's all my fault.'

Like many other writers, Mark Bradford draws a comparison with the story of Jonah: 'When the storm arrives in the Jonah story, it is because he isn't in the place that he should be.' But there is an important difference on this stormy evening on Lake Galilee as R. Alan Cole observes: 'The voyage across the lake had been undertaken at the express suggestion of Jesus, in unquestioning faith and obedience. This, for the disciples, made the coming of the storm all the harder to understand, and the relaxed attitude of Jesus quite inexplicable to them.' Cole also draws a comparison with Jonah: 'Jonah's storm, after all, had been a punishment for disobedience (Jonah 1:4), but they (the disciples) had been obedient: no wonder that they felt aggrieved at what had happened to them.' He also suggests that their waking of Jesus, shouting: 'Master, Master, we are perishing!' contains more than a hint of reproach to their sleeping passenger: 'Why had he allowed them to enter such a situation?'[xxvi]

But, as Beverley Zink-Sawyer remarks: 'Only when we have articulated those feelings – and the anger beneath them – can we be still and listen for a word from God.'[xxvii]

In the midst of the storm that is what everyone is wanting to hear.

4. Do not be afraid

'If you can keep your head when all about you are losing theirs...'[xxviii]

... Do you really understand the situation?

With apologies to Rudyard Kipling and the writer of a greeting card I saw many years ago who provided the punchline, we might think not only of the disciples with Jesus in the boat but also situations we've encountered for ourselves.

The three gospel readings phrase Jesus' response to the fear of the disciples slightly differently. In Mark, and not dissimilarly in Matthew, we read how Jesus replied: 'Why are you afraid? Have you still no faith?' In Luke, we simply have the question 'Where is your faith?'

There are some fundamental difficulties with the gospel accounts which affect our ability to see and understand them. Firstly, they are not full accounts of everything that happened in Jesus' lifetime. As John's Gospel tells us 'Jesus did many other signs in the presence of his disciples, which are not written in this book.' (John 20:30) We haven't got all the pieces of the jigsaw in order to see the picture on the box.

Secondly, we don't know everything that was said by Jesus or by others – and just as importantly, we don't know the tone in which those things were said. We are left having to interpret meaning.

In terms of Jesus' life, apart from the events in the weeks around his birth, references to when he was about two years old when visitors from the East brought gifts, and then when he was in the Temple aged 12, we know nothing else until he was 30. We know he became a carpenter (Mark 6:3) and it's likely his earthly father, Joseph died in those intervening years of young adulthood.

There are other 'gospel' accounts which didn't make it into the New Testament and they provide some indications and information about Jesus also. The four New Testament Gospels are edited versions of what was originally written: so we don't always know what was changed, taken out or added in. Similarly, the gospel writers – and the editors – will have given a particular 'spin' on the message they were conveying to their intended audience.

Like any other account, be it written, verbal or visual, our understanding also depends on how we read, listen or see: and just as importantly, how we interpret it.

'The single biggest problem in communication is the illusion that it has taken place.' Whether speaking, writing, texting, messaging or e-mailing, that wry observation (often attributed to George Bernard Shaw) remains as true today as it ever was. Shaw's words also reflect the difficulties in receiving what's been said, be that by reading, listening or seeing. We may or may not understand it – or not want to; we might hear what we think has been said – or not want to hear it; we may interpret it to mean something else – perhaps reading between the lines without having read the lines themselves; or instead of listening, we're focussing our response... 'A man hears what he wants to hear. And disregards the rest,'[xxix] as Paul Simon put it.

It's going to be OK

It took me many years to realise that when one of my children was upset, saying 'It's OK' wasn't always the right thing. 'But it's not OK, Dad!' they'd reply. From my perspective, I was trying to be reassuring. To tell them that I was with them and looking after them. That I was in some respect trying to calm the storm that had impacted upon them. But they were right. At that particular moment, it was not OK and there was no point in avoiding or denying the fact. Perhaps what I should have said was 'It's going to be OK.'

So back to interpretation. Some people have commented that they 'prefer to hold that Jesus calmed the disciples rather than the waves.'[xxx] Many commentators and preachers, and potentially most people, tend to interpret Jesus' response to the panicking disciples as being critical of them or even accusatory: 'Why are you afraid? Have you still no faith?'

Such an interpretation is reinforced by a general view that the disciples were a pretty hopeless, uneducated lot, slow to understand

and not really getting what was going on around them. Paula Gooder laments this attitude, 'Rather sadly, Christian tradition has accepted unchallenged, this prejudice and peddled it for the past 2,000 years.'[xxxi] She goes on to point out that at least four were skilled fishermen, a number would have been bi-lingual, speaking both Greek and Aramaic. Some had business acumen, other skills and abilities, and family lives to manage alongside their work and calling to follow Jesus.

Mark Bradford wonders whether Jesus was exasperated that they should have known better or, he asks, was it 'a longing, an aching within him, that they would know this greater way of faith to comprehend that even storms need not unsettle those who are with him?'[xxxii] Yes, some immediately understood that this man Jesus was special, perhaps even the long-awaited Messiah. But it was always going to take time for them to fully understand what that all meant – not least because Jesus was not the type of Messiah expected by the Jews. The disciples were still in a time of transition.

I have no doubt that, at times, Jesus was a 'difficult person' to be around – after all, it must have been pretty difficult being Jesus. Reflecting on another occasion where Jesus' words have been open to interpretation, the comedian Frank Skinner wrote in a prayer to Jesus:

> 'I find it strangely reassuring when you say wince-inducing things in the New Testament. It makes me think that the compilers had such respect for your words that they didn't dare tamper with them, even when those same words make you sound a bit spiky and thus make

their evangelising a much harder sell. That suggests that we're getting the real deal, without trims or embellishments. It gets us really close. I can almost smell the nard.'[xxxiii]

So when Jesus says 'Why are you afraid? Have you still no faith?' and we interpret it in that rather negative, critical way, what does that say about our understanding of Jesus?

Do we believe in a Jesus who speaks to the disciples like many have perhaps spoken to us in times of trouble: 'Now, don't be silly.' 'Why don't you just grow up!'? Times when we've been ridiculed for our difficulty in coping with a situation or when we've been afraid and others impose their world view upon us as to how we should react. Is that the type of Jesus we believe in?

It seems strange to think that Jesus, both man and God, the paradigm of how to love one another, should enter into the atmosphere of the disciples' own stressed and anxious language in a way that matches the tumult of the storm. Surely, would he not speak in a way that reflects the fact the storm is being calmed?

So perhaps it's helpful to think of Jesus speaking those words in a reassuring, comforting way rather than one which is interpreted as condemning the disciples for their reaction. A Jesus who understands our fear in order that he can calm it for us.

'Like the disciples, we are challenged in the midst of the storms to rediscover our faith in the promise of God's powerful word,' wrote Beverly Zink-Sawyer. 'The particular word spoken by Jesus... is a word of peace and stillness. It is a word we need to hear every day of our lives.'[xxxiv]

Michael Lindvall writes:

> 'It is important to note that Jesus never says, "There is nothing to be afraid of." The Galilean storm was doubtless indeed fearsome, as are the "wind and the waves" that threaten us... Although we often confuse them, saying "there's nothing to be afraid of,' is a very different thing from saying, "do not be afraid." The hard truth is that fearsome things are very real: isolation, pain, illness, meaninglessness, rejection, losing one's job, money problems, failure, illness, and death. As we grow in faith, we come to understand that even though such fearsome things are very real, they do not have the last word... Not because there are no fearsome things on the sea of our days, not because there are no storms, fierce winds, or waves, but rather, because God is with us.'[xxxv]

Take a moment now to bring to mind a time when you were truly afraid.

Perhaps it was a bit like the disciples in the boat. It was scary. There was no escape. You felt trapped. Maybe that happened through an accident or being attacked. Maybe it happened with the pandemic – the fear of catching Covid-19. Your job or business coming to an end. Losing a family member or friend without seeing them again.

Or maybe it was more 'subtle' than any of those. An insidious type of fear. A fear that had grown through anxiety over the years.

Which kind of Jesus would you like to hear speaking the words 'Why are you afraid?'

Pause for a while. Think back on your own life experiences. Think of your own understanding of Jesus and how others may have influenced your interpretation of his words of comfort and reassurance.

'Why are you afraid?', says Jesus, it's going to be OK.

Where is your faith?

It's the classic Authorised Kings James Version[xxxvi] that terms Jesus' words as 'Why are ye fearful, O ye of little faith?'

O ye of little faith. That ubiquitous phrase is used on just three occasions in the whole Bible – Matthew 6:30 (cf Luke 12:28), 8:26, and 16:8. Yet it occupies a place in our language that is so prominent. It's quoted at anyone who dares to raise reservations on what is possible and achievable – and any Christian who expresses doubts about the trustworthiness of God.

I imagine many of us can align ourselves with one writer's opinion about how others interpret this verse: 'Have you heard... messages where the preacher was pointing at you, making you feel like your faith was inadequate? Accusation, accusation, accusation, implying you don't measure up and that God is, if not angry at you, at least mildly disappointed.'[xxxvii]

So how are we to understand this saying of Jesus? Like the previous words, 'Why are you afraid?' it's so often been used negatively and as a loaded challenge. An accusatory 'Where is your faith?' as if it was completely absent.

Is that the Jesus we believe in?

Or is it a gentle 'It's going to be OK. Where is your faith – you can trust me. See what I can do. I can do this for you.'

Efrain Agosto reflects on the disciples and how they had heard the parable of the sower in those hours before setting off: 'Their faith still needs to grow. They act as if the seed of faith has fallen on rocky ground, such that "when trouble or persecution arises", their faith falters... They are "not yet" ready to come down completely on the side of faith.'[xxxviii] Agosto explains that by emphasising that the disciples do not yet have enough faith, the gospel writer is hopeful that one day they will.

Thinking about faith typically focuses on what it is for an individual person to 'have faith' or be 'a person of faith'. John Bishop, Professor of Philosophy at the University of Auckland, writes:

> 'An initial broad distinction is between thinking of faith just as a person's state and thinking of it as also involving a person's act, action or activity. Faith may be a state one is in, or comes to be in; it may also essentially involve something one does. An adequate account of faith, perhaps, needs to encompass both. In the Christian context, faith is understood both as a gift of

God and also as requiring a human response of assent and trust, so that their faith is something with respect to which people are both receptive and active. There is, however, some tension in understanding faith both as a gift to be received and as essentially involving a venture to be willed and enacted.'xxxix

The same writer explains that it is helpful to consider the components of faith as falling into three broad categories: the affective (a state of feeling confident and trusting), the cognitive (knowledge and revealed knowledge), and the practical (an active response).

You may like to think about how those three components make up your own faith. Are they in balance or is one component more (or less) dominant? How might that insight help you to build up your faith?

For that in many ways is what the question 'Where is your faith?' encourages us to do: to think about how we might build up our trust and confidence. How we might increase our knowledge and understanding of our faith. How we might increase our practical expressions of faith. How might we allow God to grow our faith.

Now, before you do that, remember that Jesus did not say 'And if you don't give me the right answers, I'm going to push you overboard.'

Contrary to what certain preachers say or believers think there are no pass marks on the scale called faith. It's not a competition. Yes, there may be coursework but it's not an exam.

Jesus in his love, comfort and reassurance so wants to help us stay in the boat whether the sea is stormy or calm. And he is in the boat with us. All times. All places. All weathers.

5. Other boats

Going through difficult times can be a lonely experience.

In an attempt to provide reassurance, some might tell us that 'others are in the same boat'. We might tell ourselves and others 'There are plenty worse off than me'. Whereas often it feels like we are sailing solo in a different storm.

Lonely and difficult as times of change may be, it is sometimes helpful to learn from the experiences of others as part of our finding stability within them.

In this chapter, we're going to consider what we can learn from the lives of some of those who met Jesus. In the chapter that follows, we'll hear from people living today who have shared their stories of finding stability in times of change.

The Woman of Samaria (John 4:1-42)

Fetching water was normally done in the cool of the morning or the evening. It was a community event where local women would gather to talk and be together. Yet, this unnamed woman comes alone to the well in the heat of the midday sun.

Socially unacceptable, a moral outcast, the woman of Samaria has a deep need to be loved. She has had five husbands and is now with a man who is not her husband. Whether she was repeatedly widowed or divorced (or a combination), we don't know but there is something about her that means she keeps herself safe from ridicule by walking alone at a different time of day. She feels ashamed. She has no sense of pride. Perhaps she views herself as a nobody and nobody ever speaks to her as if she was actually a somebody.

The encounter is the longest recorded conversation between a woman and Jesus in the whole of the Gospels. Initially, it has a feel of jolly repartee to it as if the woman is jesting, flirting even. After all, she has had five husbands! 'Sir, you have no bucket... the well is deep... so where do you get this living water... are you greater than Jacob?' (Nudge, nudge. Wink, wink.) But the very fact she engages in conversation reflects her deep need for love, acceptance, and respect.

Initially, Jesus responds in a calm, pragmatic way: 'Everyone who drinks this water (in the well) will be thirsty again.' (John 4:13) John records how effortlessly Jesus turns from the practical to the spiritual – 'but those who drink of the water that I will give them will never be thirsty.' (4:14)

Jesus addresses her thirst. A thirst for acceptance. A thirst for love. She's a mess. She's had five husbands. She's living with someone.

She's been excluded. Life is not good. Life is dry and she is thirsty. Life has changed – and in so many ways.

Here, now, in the heat of the midday sun, stands a man, perhaps the first man, who accepts her for who she is and who loves her because she is to be loved.

Reflecting for herself on the encounter between Jesus and the woman at the well, Rachel Frost wrote, 'He was both encouraging and challenging me to come and be in his presence. To just come. To put aside my list of questions, thoughts, and burdens that I wanted to give him, and to just come and sit with Jesus. To commune with the Father. By doing that, the Lord introduced me to the idea that what I do is to come from a place of being, to come from a place of rest and of deep refreshment. A depth of refreshment that can only come from him.'[xl]

As with the woman from Samaria, the issues we face and the difficulties we have in times of change may not go away. The woman did not go to a wishing well to find a magic wand: and Jesus didn't give her one in return for her efforts. And neither will he do so for us. But it is by going to the source of this living water, by reaching beneath the surface to the place of deep refreshment that will provide a different perspective.

We might think of ourselves as coming to the well in the heat of the different aspects of our lives. Thirsty for acceptance. Thirsty for love. Thirsty for stability. Bringing to Jesus the parts of our lives which are dry.

Nicodemus (John 3:1-21)

By contrast, Nicodemus is a respected pillar of the community – yet one who in his own way is also confused and disillusioned. John tells us how he comes to Jesus with questions, not in the midday sun but in the middle of the night. He comes seeking understanding. He comes to Jesus for direction.

Nicodemus was a leader of the Jews: the Hoi Iudaioi[xli] 'While we cannot know this for sure, it is probable that Nicodemus was a member of the Sanhedrin, the Jewish ruling council whose limited authority was sanctioned by the Roman government,' writes Israeli scholar Eli Lizorkin-Eyzenberg. 'It is obvious that Nicodemus had an uneasy connection with the Hoi Iudaioi. On the one hand, he was an intricate part of it; on the other, he was afraid and hassled by it. As such, he often felt that he did not belong.'[xlii]

It's possible that throughout his life, Nicodemus may have simply accepted all that was taught to him by the Jewish rabbis. Learning the Psalms and the Law. Listening to the story of how Moses led the children of Israel out of Egypt. Acquainting himself with the acts of Abraham, David, Elijah, Elisha and so many more. And leading others in doing the same.

But change is happening around him. Afraid to show his interest to his fellow Pharisees, Nicodemus has encountered someone who challenges all that received and perceived wisdom. A man who performs miracles. A man who is different from any other teacher he has ever known. Nicodemus knows that Jesus comes from God: he's seen the miracles ('signs' as John calls them) and we can assume he's heard the teaching.

Nicodemus came to Jesus in a state of confusion. 'It is easy to feel sympathy for Nicodemus whose questions are never really answered,' writes Laurence Cantwell. 'He came looking for an instructor and found a revealer. He came to have his learning increased and furthered and he is told he must go right back to the beginning. He came expecting a discussion on serious topics and he is issued with a personal challenge.'[xliii]

The ground under Nicodemus was shifting and he began to realise there was another way through life's events and changes: that there was more to God than he had ever thought. God will always take us to an even better place. A place of growth and depth beyond our expectations. A place of stability.

In the darkness, Nicodemus came to Jesus seeking spiritual direction. In times of our own spiritual 'darkness', it can be helpful to seek assistance from someone else to take us towards a place of stability. A guide. A companion. A wise teacher. While none of us will be able to have a spiritual guide quite the same as Nicodemus, seeking out such advice and support can be helpful.

One approach can be to have a spiritual director:

> 'Spiritual direction is a place where my story can be shared, heard, and treated as sacred. It is a process, whereby one individual (the Director) encourages another (the Directee) to reflectively embrace their story

with all its complexity – deeply inhabiting it and reflectively noticing how that story is held in a bigger story. The divine story of God's compassionate engagement with our world. In spiritual direction we are invited to cast a contemplative eye on all we are and do, opening ourselves to the possibility of transformation.'[xliv]

The Daughter of Jairus (Mark 5:22-24a, 35-43)

It's one of the most difficult experiences in life. Whatever age. Young or older. Those times when one's child is struggling or unwell – and being unable to do anything to comfort them, let alone fix it.

We don't know whether this 12 year-old girl had been unwell for a long time or whether this was a sudden onset of an acute illness. We don't know what else her parents had already done. But it seemed they had tried their best and failed. Perhaps asking for Jesus was the last resort? For Jairus, another upright citizen, a leader of the synagogue, it's a step of faith to ask an itinerant and controversial rabbi for help. You would have thought, like with the calming of the storm, Jesus would respond immediately to such an expression of faith, trust and belief. But, no, Jesus makes them wait.

When Jesus eventually arrives at Jairus' house, he is greeted by grief-stricken family and friends. They mock his 'It's OK' responses. Remember these are people who had tried their best and failed: 'But it's not OK, Jesus!'.

The daughter of Jairus needed an approach which was not nearly as 'dramatic' as the calming of Lake Galilee. When Jesus enters the room where the girl lay, he did so with just her parents and three disciples. Jesus changes the prevailing atmosphere. 'By clearing the room of an excessively noisy, grieving crowd, he brings privacy, peace, quiet, and stillness to the situation,' writes Martin Collins, who continues:

'His attention to such detail reveals his characteristic kindness and sympathy. That he orders nourishment suggests that her body was still weak and needed to be strengthened, showing that she was resurrected to physical existence. Those who saw her did not see a spirit but a human. Her body, still dependent on natural laws, needed to be nourished. Christ finishes by requesting that the parents "tell no one what had happened" (Mark 5:43; Luke 8:56), partly to save the little girl from rude gawkers, but most probably so that fame would not hinder her future spiritual life.'[xlv]

Not for her, the shouting amidst the noise of the storm but instead, calmness and quiet with those who loved her most. One size does not fit all. We see here a Jesus who responds to someone's needs in ways which are both appropriate to the situation and are exactly suited to the person concerned. This is not 'If I were you, I'd do this' – this is 'I am with you, I will do as you wish'.

And note how, just like with the calming of the storm, Mark records the reaction of those who were there in the room when they saw the girl get up and walk: 'At this they were overcome with amazement.' (Mark 5:42)

Thomas (John 20: 24-29)

Thomas was one of Jesus' closest friends. A dedicated companion. Going everywhere and seeing everything. Thomas was one who sought to understand who Jesus was and what his purpose was. He asked questions when Lazarus was reported dead (John 11:16) and again in the minutes that followed Judas' departure from the Last Supper (John 14:1-6). Three years spent in such company. And yet despite all that, we might say, he had doubts.

So here we have 'Doubting Thomas'. A term sometimes used derogatively towards those who don't believe or agree with what others might be proposing. The phrase even has its own dictionary definitions: 'an incredulous or habitually doubtful person';[xlvi] 'a person who insists on proof before he or she will believe anything; sceptic'.[xlvii] And yet we can learn a lot from Thomas.

'Thomas was not afraid to express his doubt – for that is how he really feels,' writes David Adam.[xlviii] He is, as Serene Jones puts it, 'The incredulous nonbeliever who hides inside every believing Christian – the questioner in us that resists easy answers to hard questions of faith, who always wants a little more proof.'[xlix]

Or as David Stone put it:

> 'People troubled by doubts are often plagued by a feeling of guilt that their faith isn't strong enough. Doubts can become enmeshed in a conspiracy of silence that makes it difficult to be open about them. We try and sit on our doubts and hang on grimly to an apparently cheerful but actually rather unreal faith. It can be hard to admit that

we have doubts and to ask the difficult questions that we feel guilty about having. But it really is no good to tell ourselves "Just believe!" and brush the problems under the carpet.'[l]

Left unaddressed or unresolved, doubts can become all-consuming – like a strong wind over the waves. They have the power to erode away confidence in our ability to make decisions. To the extent that we never make any at all. We can also find ourselves holding on to doubts even with the greatest evidence to the contrary. Paradoxically, having doubts is one thing in life we can be certain about.

'Thomas, with his scepticism, is a good model for Christians,' writes Jennifer Brown. 'Yes, we need to have faith, but faith is not believing without evidence or without questioning. We should have the courage and the confidence to ask questions and to explore the evidence. Only then will we be able to provide a robust explanation of our faith to others.' Comparing him to a scientist, she continues: 'He wanted to test the evidence for himself, he wanted to run his own experiment if you like. And, when he saw that the evidence did, in fact, support the theory – hard to believe though it was – he accepted it.'[li]

We, with all our doubts, come to Christ in the knowledge that we have not seen him. We come to Christ in faith, trusting that, in the balance of probability, he is alive and he is with us. He takes those doubts, that faith, and that trust and blesses us. And provides a sense of stability amidst the doubts and the difficulties.

In our desire (and perhaps pressure) to understand everything (combined with a sense of guilt that if we have doubts then somehow our faith isn't good enough), we can lose some of the non-rational mystery of faith. I know for me, my rational thinking challenges many of the non-rational aspects of belief: so much so, at times, I could quite easily not believe – and part of the mystery of faith is that I continue to choose to do so.

Thomas believed because he met the risen Christ, whereas, we are blessed with being able to do so without seeing him. (John 20:26-29)

How else can we respond but by saying 'My Lord and my God!'

And how good is that?

Mary Magdalene (John 20:11-18)

Like many of us after a bereavement, Mary Magdalene visited the place where her loved one was laid. It was night. She knew she could go there in peace to pay her respects, to mourn, to talk to the one she had lost, to be in that person's presence even though they are dead: there is something reassuring about being able to do so – it keeps that deep emotional connection.

But on that first Easter morning, as the sun was rising upon the darkened land, Mary didn't find what she expected. The stone carefully placed over the entrance to the tomb by Nicodemus and Joseph of Arimathea, whom she had watched, had been moved (Matt 27:57-61). The body had gone. What loss – and then this.

No doubt, as she sat weeping, Mary recalled Jesus' teaching about his death and resurrection. And yet the body had gone. Even the appearance of angels did not bring consolation. A gardener came and she poured out her distress to him. What on earth was going on?

And then one word changed everything. A word charged with emotion. A word which encapsulated all she was, covered all her confusion and distress and brought together all her faith and hope.

'Mary.'

In this one word, the simple utterance of her name, Mary found the Lord. And her Lord found her. Mary had found the true fulfilment of who God had made her to be. She hears her name and says his in reply.

When someone calls our name, it attracts our attention. We turn to face them. We respond to the voice. We recognise the person who says it. Hearing our name spoken makes us turn in the right direction. And if we are looking for someone we've lost, we might call out their name. And such is the joy when we find them – and such is the joy of the person who has been found.

Through the resurrection, Jesus calls each one of us by name.

Through the resurrection, each one of us can find what we are looking for.

Why not take a few minutes to listen to the voice of Jesus calling your name?

Bartimaeus (Mark 10:46-51)

Bartimaeus, a blind beggar sitting by the road in the city of Jericho hears Jesus approaching. He calls out and, miraculously, his sight is restored. Suddenly, everything changed. And what a change: an instantaneous one too. It must have been both thrilling and disconcerting – suddenly seeing all that light, all the people ('like trees walking', as the blind man of Bethsaida described it in his similar healing [Mark 8:22-26]).

For Bartimaeus, it was his faith in Jesus that enabled him to see clearly. But it wasn't just about that. That encounter is also about the question Jesus asked Bartimaeus: 'What do you want me to do for you?'

Imagine for a moment, Jesus asking you that question:

'What do you want me to do for you?'

Possibly, like many people, you may have a very long list of answers. You may be thinking, 'Well, I've asked you to do lots of things which haven't happened.' Our unanswered answers are tough at times...

It can be difficult to hold that apparent absence of response in tension with things Jesus promised: 'Ask, and it will be given to you' (Matthew 7:7) '...if you do not doubt in your heart, but believe that what you say will come to pass, it will be done for you. So I tell you, whatever you ask for in prayer, believe that you have received it, and it will be yours.' (Mark 11:23-24)

Bartimaeus received what he wanted Jesus to do for him. And afterwards... yes, he could see again. Many would be amazed by his miraculous healing. But he may well have remained a beggar and an outcast. And people would still tell him to shut up.

But perhaps, despite all that, his faith remained strong.

It can be like that for us: we receive some of what we want, while other things remain difficult.

Peter (Matthew 14:22-33)

Another storm on Lake Galilee. Out of the tumult, Jesus walks on the water towards the disciples in their tossed-about boat. Given their exhaustion and the darkness, it's not surprising they think it's a ghost.

But Peter knows it's Jesus. Responding to Christ's call, Peter steps out in faith on to the water... and then he noticed the wind.

Peter sinks down and is grasped by Jesus' hand. Jesus climbs in the boat and calms the storm, allowing the disciples to continue their journey.

Stepping out in faith is no guarantee that we will not hit troubled or stormy waters. As already considered, you may have had your own encounters with stepping out in faith and things being difficult. Times when you stepped out... and noticed the wind.

Jesus said to Peter: 'You of little faith, why did you doubt?' Those words again.

Did Peter really have little faith? After all, nobody else got out of the boat.

So here too, are we. We of little faith. A little faith that enables us to step out in the storm. A faith which grasps the hand of Jesus as he reaches out to us.

Jesus places us safely in the boat. He climbs in with us. He calms the storm and takes us on our journey. A journey yes, into uncharted waters. A journey of continuing change. But also a journey of certainty because we will never be allowed to drown.

Whatever the change. Whatever the loss of certainty. Do not be afraid.

*   *   *

You may like to look at some other examples of what we can learn from people who knew Jesus at astorytotell.org.uk

6. Other people

'Wherever there are people, there are problems,' someone said to me many years ago.

Over the course of more than 35 years of helping people to find or remain in employment and specialising in supporting those experiencing mental ill health, I also came to discover that wherever there are people, there is hope; wherever there are people, there is progress; wherever there are people, there is companionship.

I am so grateful to the people who have contributed their accounts of problems, hope, progress and companionship to this book. All have given their permission for their stories to be used, they are included verbatim (slightly edited for length in places) and some asked to remain anonymous.

These are their accounts of finding stability (or not) in times of change. Stories of retirement and employment, illness and loss, comfort and solace. They tell of the lives of the lay and the ordained. Some are a challenging read, but I hope you will find encouragement in the knowledge of how others encounter storms and, especially, how they have come through them.

Vanessa Dixon

'The transition from work to retirement has been a profound change, which has triggered a series of further changes in the last decade of my life. I know that I was fortunate in being able to choose to retire early. My husband, Malcolm, had retired ahead of me and encouraged me to do the same. After having children, I had only ever worked part-time, as full-time work in veterinary practice meant long hours and nights on call. I had experienced this earlier in my career and didn't consider it to be compatible with family life. I enjoyed my work in a local small animal practice, where I'd been for 17 years. However, there were some factors that made me feel that the time was right to close that chapter of my life: ageing joints and the frequent need to grovel on the floor with large and uncooperative dogs, being one such factor!

'I made my decision during a residential retreat at St Mary's Abbey, West Malling. I was reading Robert Atwell's book, The Contented Life: Spirituality and the Gift of Years.[lii] This helped me to see that retirement was potentially a fruitful time. I talked through the decision that was looming over me with the retreat conductor, and that conversation helped me to crystallise my thoughts and prayers. Although I had taken a career break while our children were very small, I believed that my work as a vet supplied a key part of my identity, so I was apprehensive about who I would become in retirement.

'Around the same time, Malcolm and I were making a long slow, mutual decision that we should move churches. This was after 27 years of worshipping at a traditionalist Anglo-Catholic church, where our two daughters had been baptised and confirmed. We loved the liturgy there, but as Affirming Catholics we found the separatism, particularly in relation to episcopal oversight, increasingly difficult to take. The change of church came some months after my retirement. The impact of both retirement and the move to join a different church was in both cases (in the short term at least) one of a sense of release and relief.

'My faith has been nourished by monastic links for many years, and I am profoundly thankful for it. My monastic links are specifically with CR: the Community of the Resurrection, based at Mirfield in West Yorkshire. This link, via the Companion's Rule, has been a source of stability for me, in spite of wobbliness on my part! When time off permitted, visits to stay at Mirfield with my stabilising monks, with their lives of regular prayer and worship, continued to encourage me in the life of faith. The framework of daily prayer and the requirement of a yearly retreat of some kind has become more important than ever to me in retirement. These are the faith routines that stabilise, but the requirements of a Rule also lead me to new places on my journey. The encouragement of some secular involvement has led me to outdoor volunteering in our nearby nature reserve and also volunteering at our local foodbank. These have both led in turn to new conversations and new friendships. CR's stress on ecumenism led me to volunteer as secretary of our local Churches Together. All of this emanates from Benedictine stability!'

Andrew Norman, Counsellor & Priest

'I was ordained in the Church of England in 1978 when I was in my mid-twenties. I served two curacies in the Canterbury Diocese which were both very happy and developmentally positive experiences. I was then appointed as an incumbent in a small rural parish where I stayed for nine years. During this time I also served part-time as a hospital chaplain, oversaw post-ordination training in the diocese for a couple of years, and completed a doctoral degree at London University. By then I was married and we had two small children. As the eldest reached school age I looked for a move. I saw a post advertised which seemed to tick all my boxes. So I applied, was rigorously interviewed, and was then overjoyed to be appointed. Then followed a further period of twenty-seven years which again were both very happy for us as a family and completely fulfilling for me as a priest. However, towards the end of this time, while still enjoying ministry I was increasingly feeling over-burdened, constrained, and that I had less energy. I said privately to Himself, and admitted only to my wife: "While it has been very good, I now honestly feel that I've just had enough." I was nearing the age when retirement would be possible and that began to seem an attractive option.

'Everything then seemed to fall then into place. We inherited a small house in Devon near where some of our family lived. Despite the difficulties caused by the pandemic, we managed to move in the summer of 2020. I knew I would personally find the move very difficult as it had taken me a long while to settle after our last relocation. This time I would be losing my role as a parish priest, letting go of so many relationships; we would have to down-size in a major way (we had accumulated a vast amount in our very large Rectory), and I would be moving away from the part of the country where I had spent my whole life. During the first few weeks in Devon, I felt dazed but happy. Yet within me, I felt three persistent questions: Where are we? Who am I now? What should I be doing?

'Fortunately, I had started asking myself that last question a few years before retirement. The answer that came was that I felt drawn to counselling as corresponding to the personal support and listening aspect of pastoral ministry to which I felt most attuned. I pushed at this door and found that it opened. A local Further Education college offered a course which would take me to become qualified. Some financial help to pay the fees emerged. The diocese was happy for me to take some time out to undertake the three-year part-time training. The course itself, with my own required therapy, turned out to involve deep self-exploration. It also felt very energising. Although I had not taken this route to help with the big transition of retirement that was exactly what it did for me. Almost two years later I am now living out the answer to that third question. I spend two days a week in therapeutic work on a voluntary basis and have the rest of the week to develop some private practice - but I am free to regulate the amount of time I allow for that according to what feels the right balance for me. I think of it as an authentic evolution of my priestly vocation (though a priestly identity is now almost completely implicit and invisible). It gives me a sense of purpose which I find very stabilising. As time goes on my ability to access the freedom from full-time ministry is growing. Six years ago I became a Quaker and began to establish a new balance between that emphasis on simplicity, silence, integrity and the outward expression of my catholic preferences. I swung strongly back to the latter as my coping strategy in the first pandemic lockdown, but I now feel able to let the former re-assert itself. I am very much finding my stability in that spiritual balance and valuing the freedom which allows for it.'

Dr Barbara Duncan

'Working as a volunteer with Hospice Africa Uganda on and off over 8 years after retirement from the NHS, I also took on an MSc in Palliative Care to inform me about the sphere of work I was volunteering for. International flights on a regular basis were disruptive so planning flights carefully to ease time transition was important. Once back in Uganda or UK getting back to a routine of Lauds and meditation in the morning and Vespers and meditation after work was key to settling into wherever I was. Also, when I needed a break I would go and sit at a quiet table in the country club across the road from the Hospice, have tea or coffee, put on my headphones & listen to the day's meditation from 'Pray as You Go'. I also tried to keep tuning into God to discern whether I was doing what God wanted me to do. I also needed a church in both places that became familiar to me. That was more difficult in Uganda but I settled on Namirembe Cathedral. In London, that's when I discovered Southwark Cathedral. It was always exciting to return for services there. When in Uganda I'd go to church at 7am and enjoy listening to sermons from Southwark Cathedral to keep in touch with them. I enjoyed my Sunday mornings! I'm an oblate of Malling

Abbey so following their office as above was key to feeling grounded & connected.'

God isn't going anywhere

'My husband was diagnosed with bowel cancer and had to undergo major surgery and 6 months of chemotherapy. I had just been ordained Deacon and was obviously still in training. I took unpaid leave from my job as a Chaplain in a London hospital, and from the church, and ongoing training was required. Everything was up in the air but the main person I needed to concentrate on was my husband. Our grown-up children were a wonderful support, and I felt the support of the church I had joined - and my incumbent, although he was heading for a breakdown but he gave what he could. I had a very good spiritual director who I talked to on the telephone as I was so busy providing care after the operation, and he was someone who worked with those who were in the NHS and I felt had had an experience of deep loss so compassionate was his voice through the various emergencies that occurred. Physically I was totally exhausted but did find just enough strength for each day, and I used to read Richard Rohr's daily meditations which helped enormously. Because my home life was abusive, I also had a wonderful therapist (also a Christian) who guided my path.

'Daily prayer - morning and evening were stable points of the day, as were friends and family. My therapist was as ever wonderful. The Marsden was a wonderful place to be, and the doctors there were so supportive. My incumbent called regularly to pray with us and anoint my husband. We had a friend who was both a priest and mental health lead chaplain, who was very supportive and telephoned regularly with helpful thoughts. His practical guidance as well as spiritual and emotional input was quite invaluable. He was a strong place to be real with at the end of the 'phone whenever I needed. Sometimes I couldn't pray and my incumbent said to me "Don't worry, God isn't going anywhere."'

Unconditionally loved

'As a naval child, I moved homes and schools frequently and until adulthood didn't realise how much constant moves both in the UK and abroad affected friendships and ability to ask for help. I don't look to any place as home and find the question, "Where are you from?" impossible to answer simply. As an adult the experience of moving and flexibility and ability to just on wherever I was, was a strength for life as a clergy wife, needing to move often, get on with new people and be able to cope with unusual experiences. About six years ago, one of my children transitioned gender and we have been supporting her through this major change to our family life.

'My faith helped us through this as we needed to learn more about gender transition and to open our hearts in love to both our own child and also others in a similar situation. Faith was also difficult as well, as we faced questions from other Christians (some friends walked away, others accepting) and having to tell extended family, who were unexpectedly supportive. I still have lots of questions and wish life had been easier for her but know that our love for our daughter is strong and also overwhelmed by a deepened understanding of God's wonderful unconditional love too.'

Stopping & starting

'In January 2019 I left parochial ministry in one diocese to take up a different kind of ministerial role in another, as an archdeacon and also as a cathedral canon. This involved change in every part of my life. The context for ministry was different – much more of an oversight role. I would be leaving behind the settled community represented by multi-parish ministry and many of the things I loved – especially the deeply incarnational work of walking alongside people through life events of every kind. Despite the many challenges of parochial ministry I would be embarking on what felt to me like a particularly demanding role, certainly out of my comfort zone. Much of what I would be doing would be new to me and require learning new skills and gaining fresh experience. This move also involved leaving behind the only diocese I had ever served in, my home county and many friends and family members. I would also be living in a city again for the first time in many years. I remember a whole range of emotions – excitement, anticipation, anxiety, fear of failure, sadness, loss and gratitude. I also remember great extremes of emotion – being completely overwhelmed by the love and care manifested at my leaving service and in the way people said goodbye. And then a wonderful welcome as we arrived in our new home. And, in those early days of a new role, the affirmation of licensing and collation, the overwhelming amount of new information, the geographical challenge of finding my way around a new county and the sheer number of people to get to know. For much of the time, I was exhausted and often felt inadequate, wondering if I would ever feel on top of the roles to which I had been appointed. And then, all of a sudden, our new home felt familiar, the days settled into some kind of rhythm, relationships formed and this new ministry seemed more rewarding, and less scary. I felt less of a novice.

'As ever, the moments of ritual were so important in coping with the move I experienced. The service of farewell which so many of us dread and which we might be tempted to avoid has such value. It represents a proper goodbye – an acknowledgement of where we have fallen short and where we have done our best; a sharing of precious memories; an expression of feelings; an articulation of loss and hope. And then arriving here, the service of welcome marked a proper start to a new life. At the very beginning, a head teacher from the benefice 'handed me over' with words of introduction to my new friends and colleagues. Again, I often look back to that moment with huge gratitude. As the service progressed so the focus properly shifted to the work I was called to do next, and those with whom I would share it. Stability came from working out what helps me to flourish and ensuring it was in place. The daily office had been a key feature of benefice life - and it fell naturally into place through my cathedral role. The stable community that means so much to me would be central once again - a great blessing in the otherwise itinerant life of an archdeacon. Gradually I learned to incorporate what makes my heart sing in ministry into my new role – an emphasis on relationships and pastoral care; teaching – which led to involvement both in working with curates and a focus on schools' work; liturgy and preaching which are at the heart of archidiaconal ministry anyway. All of this has informed and sustained the statutory parts of my role. I recognised it was important for me to nurture other foundational parts of my life: prayer, reading, study. Regular time with my spiritual director, retreats and quiet days. Days off and holidays. And gradually I needed to learn to trust those around me. I needed to make mistakes, ask for help and have the confidence and security to have a bad day, knowing that it would not be seen as failure. Away from work I also recognised the need to maintain stability by spending time with family and friends (old and new), enjoying the things that bring me life – music, reading, walking, gardening, travel. After a relatively short time in a new place and a new role the Covid 19 pandemic struck. I can honestly say this has been the most difficult time of my life. Finding stability in such a time has been immensely challenging. As for so many others, these months have brought bereavement, illness, loneliness, isolation, despair, sleeplessness and fear. My sense of stability has been stretched to the limit. My salvation has been a ministry I love and feel privileged to exercise and, above all, the humanity, kindness, tenderness and love of those whose lives touch mine.'

Wherever I am

'So many changes that were very overwhelmingly awful... A lot of sadness and pain in the first half of my life made it hard to maintain work, relationships etc. However, I found some relief by travelling. I now want to focus on a recent positive change which has been finding my voice and creativity via writing. Since Covid 19, I have found both community and space with other writers. This is nourishing, empowering and uniting.

'There are times when parish church drains me and I often have to walk in the hills and by the coast to find peace. I have to step back from church emotionally... but am delighted to write the intercessions and contribute. Don't always find local church a sanctuary to 'be' and have to protect my energy. This makes me sad when I am low and in need of a pick-me-up. Hence the writers are a Godsend (many of whom may not be church-going Christians) I live alone and am single... at present 'non sexually active' heterosexual woman aged 56 and often feel overlooked and overshadowed by those with busy jobs and grandchildren etc, etc. As a single person, I find it crucially important to be discerning about who to trust, particularly within a church, in order to thrive in the second half of life. As much as the church says it is inclusive, status is often on those who are married or single male. I learn to navigate and look after myself and then it's OK wherever I am.'

Lance Pierson, Actor

Like all the contributors to this book, Lance wrote his account in May 2021.

'Three years ago I had a heart attack. I was whisked to hospital where a surgeon inserted two stents, and I survived. After three days I was able to go home but was summoned to a weekly rehab course of exercises. At the end of those ten weeks, we were advised to go on to a more advanced weekly club. This is a group of about 20 of us, who call ourselves 'The Heart-throbs'. We have become firm friends and it is a highlight of my week; six of them share my Christian faith. I do 10 minutes of those exercises each day between classes. I also do a vigorous cycle ride for at least 30 minutes each day. At the same time as exercising more, I eat less - one course less at breakfast and supper; no puddings at lunch, only fruit; and no snacks between meals! I have lost two stones and shed some aches and pains in the process. Mercifully I am still able to work but have reduced the number of pies my fingers are in, and try to work only three days a week. I suspect I am healthier now than for many years before I was ill.

'After the heart attack, I had four months of great uncertainty (several tests and muddled appointments) before I finally saw the specialist who told me, to my enormous surprise and relief, that I was well again and could resume normal (but sensible!) life. In the meantime, I had very nervously driven the car when my wife needed a rest; now the specialist told me that under no circumstances was I to report my illness to the DVLA, as they would remove my licence - quite unnecessarily! Various of my employers had made no allowance for my illness and still expected me to travel across the country to attend meetings. I set off very early and walked slowly to catch trains. I acted in a play where I had to jump - this was such a shock to the system that I wondered if I had dislodged a stent. All the time I expected each twinge to be the onset of another attack and prayed fervently that God would see me through at least to fulfil my existing commitments. He has done so and restored far greater stability. But the realisation that each day, each job, each conversation might be my last is a good discipline that I try to teach myself to remember.'

Sadly, Lance died in October 2021 from cancer which was not expected at all. His wife, Sue told me about how on hearing the diagnosis of his illness, Lance planned his funeral, which his family turned into a service of thanksgiving for his life. Over 200 people came to the service wearing bright colours and another 80 households watched online. An actor, writer, speaker and trainer, he was also the National Chairman of the John Betjeman Society. Many people were grateful for having known him.

I am very grateful to Sue for both her permission and her desire to include Lance's contribution in this book so others may continue to benefit from his life.

God the creator

'I retired from paid work in October 2019. l immediately became involved with preparation for my being a witness at an Employment Tribunal for my employer. My brother suddenly died in January 2020. Employment Tribunal attendance for a week in March, followed 7 days later by lockdown. Major life changes and bereavement.

'I realise that my having a box of rescued vegetables each week has paid a major role in my recovery. I was and am contributing to keeping farmers going when their major customers (restaurants) were disappearing. I had to use up vegetables which supermarkets rejected as not meeting size and appearance standards. I was using vegetables I have never bought before (ugly vegetables, celeriac). I am cooking every day using new recipes to nurture myself. I now realise that I have a better relationship with food - more mindful, slower eating more appreciation. I listen more and speak less. I have also lost 17lbs so feel able to take care of myself in other ways (friends, health, renovating my house). I have also saved water, energy and carbon by saving food from going into compost. I have worked through lockdown, major changes in everyday life and losing my brother. I feel linked to God's creation in a new, closer way and so with God the creator.'

Revd Frank Wright, Retired Priest

'Retirement. Churchwise (Anglican) one becomes a no-one, unable to hold any office, not even be on the electoral roll. After a while, new roles emerge as one finds people and activities to engage with, perhaps through volunteering and having time to serve with charities. Not wearing a dog collar means people do not speak in the street unless you have met them in some context. One realises that one can be 'troublesome' without worrying. It is a big change and cannot really be prepared for (what can?). I had to answer the question, 'Who am I now?' becoming conscious of having to be me and not someone in role.

'By establishing a daily and weekly routine of sorts and becoming involved with the local community. By accepting the limitations ageing brings - ouch!'

Lifelong shadows

'I was 10 when my mother died unexpectedly, and in front of me, from a massive heart attack. To describe the moment and the knock-on effects would take too long but the upshot was that our grandmother moved in and shortly after we went to a boarding school which we could not really afford. Within the space of a year, my home life had been utterly disrupted. Looking back the main effects were two. Firstly, a long-term numbness which halted any sense of proper grieving. I do not blame my father for this, he was a broken man. Secondly, I developed an unhealthy work ethic which drove me to excel. I knew how much the school was costing, I knew we didn't have the money, and I was determined to be an A-grade student to justify the expense. The damage from both these has been long-term. All the counselling and therapy since have helped but I still find myself lapsing back into unhealthy patterns of life and work imbalance. Eventually, I moved to a part-time role to redress the balance. Bringing up my own children was done with a fierce determination for their lives to be different - however old habits run deep and I think I have passed something of my scarring on to them. However, I have a determination that the grief of children needs to be considered and allowed which has informed my ministry ever since.

'Spiritually though it was a different story. My mum was a person of faith and brought us up as Christians. Her death deepened my faith, and talking to God became vital. I needed God to be real and heaven to be more so. I also know, despite what churches sometimes tell me, that children and young people can be deeply spiritual and have innate faith. Nurturing what is there is important.

'I have described above how faith grew in the wake of my mother's death. There was something stabilising about securing the disruption in the hands of a God who was bigger than it all. I have been angry at God many times, but never about my mum. Even as I type that it seems odd! But perhaps there is a key here, I allow all the rawness of feeling to be expressed in the safety of prayer. Stuff I bottle up in human interaction can be laid out before God. I love the psalms and introduce others to them, sometimes before the gospels. Being real before God is so important to me. Freedom to think, ask questions and have doubts. All of these have grown out in the aftermath of my mother's death. At University I found a college chaplain who positively encouraged this open exploration and did not try to package faith into one neat parcel.

'I 'get' Ecclesiastes and strangely it is the ambiguity of that text which brings me stability. Marriage and children brought physical security and safety - no one was going to 'send me away' anymore. That has been so important. I still feel slightly sick in September and have nightmares during the exam season of June but now someone is there to reassure me. My main point is that changes in childhood can have far-reaching effects and, when I was a nipper, didn't receive the attention they deserved. I would want to hope that attitudes are different now.'

Catherine

'In my parish life, I came to my current benefice partly because there was the support of four retired clergy and a nearly full-time associate colleague. I'd had a lonely first incumbency with ill-health problems so support seemed essential when looking for a new post. Two-and-a-half years after I arrived, they had all disappeared. Not because of poor relationships with me, but to move house or because they became too frail to continue. Emotionally, this was a very difficult time. I live alone and the nature of ministry is that I have few local friends; my family all live far away. It left me feeling isolated and panicky about how I would cope with the future, and scared that my previous health problems would return. And practically it increased my workload a lot as there were fewer people to share many of the priestly tasks with. It also meant big changes in the Sunday service offerings we could make across the four churches. Leading such big changes was new to me, and I desperately wanted to take people with me and not fall out with them.

'I ensured that I kept in place the things I knew helped me to stay on an even keel - regular exercise written into the diary, sensible bedtimes (even when I didn't sleep well), always taking my weekly day off and holiday allowance. Beginning the discipline of centering prayer each day, although some time after this big change, has also made an enormous difference to my everyday resilience. A while after they all departed, I ended up having some time off for exhaustion. That was a wake-up call and helped me to accept that putting in place what I needed to stay healthy and well was an essential, not a luxury and would benefit my ministry rather than detract from it, even if it meant making less time in the diary for all the work commitments. Encouraging and building up a team of lay people to lead worship enabled us to re-jig the Sunday services. There were things people had to let go of and changes for them, but those big changes now just seem a normal part of parish life. A big change was in my own attitude - learning that there may be things I needed to let go of myself, that doing everything was just not possible, and that saying so did not mean I was a failure, but an ordinary human being with limits.'

Julia

'In January 2020, my mum was diagnosed with end-stage pancreatic cancer with only a few months left to live. Losing my mum was something I had dreaded ever since I could remember. We had always been incredibly close and had kept that tight bond even though I was now married with two children. She had always been my best friend, my counsellor, my support, my confidant, my spiritual mentor and had showered me with unconditional love from the day I was born. The thought of losing her rocked my very foundations; a feeling of being anchorless. On top of this bewilderment were feelings of guilt and regret. I was a nurse practitioner: why had alarm bells not rung earlier? Why had I readily agreed with her reasonings as to why she was losing the weight she was or experiencing the lack of appetite? Why hadn't I insisted she went to the GP's sooner? Only two weeks after learning the awful news, I managed to deeply impale my foot on a loose iron railing whilst out running, requiring two operations. During that hospital stay, I had to battle with an overwhelming sense of loss of control and uncertainty. The only slight benefit is the trauma took my mind off my mum to some extent.

'By this time the Covid pandemic was upon us and so seeing her had to be either through an open window or, when the weather allowed, out in the garden. Those times were precious but incredibly painful. I knew what was coming and just to watch her deteriorate day by day without being able to change anything was agonising. It was so difficult to have a 'normal' conversation whilst the huge elephant was sitting there in the corner. I wanted to be with her but I hated to be with her - it was too painful. I needed to talk with her about how dreadful I felt about the situation and yet didn't want to selfishly burden her with my broken heart. I stepped into nurse mode at this point, which at least made me feel as though I was helping practically and it kept me busy and focused. I had nursed dying patients before but to be in that role for someone so close and so dear was pretty traumatic. She passed away in May 2020. I was there when it happened with my dad and sister. I closed her eyes.

'Of course, it's never just the earthquake of change that has to be dealt with but the tsunami that often follows. My younger sister particularly was totally devastated and needed a lot of support and time in the following months. My dad also needed a lot of help - more from a practical stance than an emotional one: for the first time in his life he was having to plan and cook meals, sort his own laundry and manage the housework. The pandemic, of course, exacerbated things in that I could not go physically into the house to help or have him round for meals and, of course, all the usual hobbies and social links which would have supported both my dad and sister had all been stopped.

'Although I had always had a faith, the process of losing mum had abruptly demonstrated to me that she, more than God, had been the rock and foundation of my life thus far. Ironically my church's verse of the year was Psalm 62:5-6 which I found incredibly powerful and relevant: 'For God alone my soul waits in silence, for my hope is from Him, He alone is my rock and my salvation, my fortress; I shall not be shaken.' I memorised this and kept repeating it to myself. The first few days, weeks and months after mum's death I found myself craving solitude; time to process; time alone with God; silence. In this respect I was glad of lockdown - I need make no excuse not to see people. During this time I was blessed to be reading a book by Richard Foster: Celebration of Discipline. It helped me re-orientate myself away from my present circumstances and onto God. I developed a daily prayer, meditation and study time to start my day which help

ed provide stability and a constant drip-effect to focus my thoughts beyond the temporal. It also prompted me to focus on other people's needs, trying to serve God through serving them, whether it be through conversations, practical help or prayers. I felt a great sense of peace, stillness, strength and love that I couldn't have imagined possible during this turbulent time. I literally felt carried in God's arms. I had placed my sadness, my fears, my trauma, my weakness at the Lord's feet, with total resignation to God's overall plan and will. The settled knowledge that God was in charge gave my heart a stillness. I also found that surrounding myself with nature very healing at this time; weeding, planting, pruning; observing, smelling, touching and listening - all imbuing a sense of God's over-riding majesty in creation. All in a process of change. Season after season. Life and then death and again life, in a new form.

*　　*　　*

It's hard watching from the shore, isn't it? Seeing people go through storms. Feeling compassion, pain, and sometimes, helplessness. Getting annoyed at the lack of a quick fix or when no other help is available. It may be that we're in the same boat as them – which can be both helpful and unhelpful. And how tempting it is to shout in the storm: 'If only you'd listened to me...' And of course, that is understandable – albeit not the most helpful thing to say. We've all had times when we could have listened to others but chose to sail on in our own sweet way...

Sometimes we have to let people ride out the storm by themselves because we can no longer cope. Hard as it sounds, we may need to watch and wait for someone to get to a point of being like the disciples and asking for help. (It's also very easy for our 'caring' to be complicit with the negative impact of the events affecting our loved ones.) We might have tried our best to calm the storm but quite often it's the person themselves who has to want to do so.

It is often the acknowledgment of difficulty and the act of choosing to proactively make a change that helps find stability. And that applies equally to those of us who travel with them.

7. Who then is this?

In his life on earth, Jesus experienced his own times of change: so let's have a look at how he found stability...

In the Temple (Luke 2.41-52)

As mentioned before, we know very little about Jesus' life before he was aged 30. But one significant moment happened when he was 12 years old, in the Temple.

'The purpose of the coming to Jerusalem,' writes G Campbell Morgan, 'was undoubtedly primarily that of fulfilling the requirements of the law, the bringing of Jesus to his confirmation... The rite, which is still in existence, consists of the preparation by the candidate of certain passages of the law, which are to be recited, and his presentation to the rulers and doctors, that in conversation with him, they may ask him questions, testing his knowledge, and he may submit to them questions arising out of his training.'[liii]

Having spent family time in Jerusalem for the festival of the Passover, Joseph and Mary set off home to Nazareth - a journey of about 64 miles. This was a time when families and travellers intermingled with ease and without fear, being looked after and fed by others. It's also fair to speculate that their other children, being younger, probably distracted their parents from realising the absence of the eldest. At the evening stopping point, Mary and Joseph started to look for Jesus among the others who were with them... 'Oh, no! We've lost the Messiah!'

So, they set off back to Jerusalem – a day's walk and another three whole days pass before they actually find him. Can you imagine losing someone (or being lost) for three whole days? Bad enough when it's three whole minutes.

And when they do find him, their reaction is natural: 'Child...' Oh dear, watch out Jesus, you are in big, big trouble. 'Child, why have you treated us like this?' they said. 'Look...' (another 'parents are really angry' word), 'Look, your father and I have been searching for you in great anxiety.' (Luke 2:48) Don't you just love the sanitised version Luke gives us!

While there would have been other 12 year-olds who went to the Temple to be questioned by the teachers, Jesus already seems to know he's different. It may be that he has been told by Mary and Joseph about his miraculous conception, the flight to Egypt and the visit of the travellers but inwardly he knew this was not just the Temple: it was his Heavenly Father's house.

He knew where he was. The Temple was already a point of stability for him even at that young age. It was a place that was important to him – a point perhaps emphasised by the pain he experienced in the same place, some 20 years later:

> 'Jesus entered the temple and began to drive out those who were selling and those who were buying in the temple, and he overturned the tables of the money-changers and the seats of those who sold doves; and he would not allow anyone to carry anything through the temple. He was teaching and saying, 'Is it not written, "My house shall be called a house of prayer for all the nations"? But you have made it a den of robbers.' (Mark 11:15-17)

Our modern-day churches contain that same mixture of stability and instability. We may or may not like all that goes on there – whether that is tradition, worship styles or people. But there is still a place for the Church, a gathering for believers and non-believers alike. A place which with all its faults provides a sense of stability when times are changing.

In what ways does the church aid your stability?

In the wilderness (Matt 4:1-11; Mark 1:12-13; Luke 4:1-13)

When the Holy Spirit led Jesus into the wilderness it was another time of change.

By their very nature, wildernesses are barren places. But in this particular wilderness, there would have been sources of fresh water and some areas of forest with other nutrients. Just like his cousin, John the Baptist, Jesus probably ate the odd locust or two and I imagine he would have already learned which plants were safe to eat. This 30 year-old man's basic needs would have been met even if it wasn't totally what he wanted.

Amidst the hunger, tiredness and barrenness, the Devil tried to mess with Jesus' mind and his mission and tempted him three times: (1) 'You must be hungry... turn these stones in to bread.' (2) 'You think you are so powerful... and you can prove it, can't you? Go on, jump!' (3) 'Worship me – and I'll give you everything in the world!' These were challenging and dangerous days for the one about to set off on his journey of ministry – a journey for which he already knew the destination.

Describing God as being like a mother hen protecting her brood from a marauding fox, Nadia Bolz-Weber once said, 'The mother hen offers us a place of shelter and love so we know where we belong. The fox still exists. The danger is not optional. The fear is. Under the protective wings, we are loved.'[liv]

Jesus knew he was protected and loved. That is where stability lies.

How do you know you are protected and loved in wilderness times?

In solitary places

One of the most familiar ways in which Jesus found stability in times of change was when he went off on his own to pray.

In between healing a number of people in his early ministry, Mark records how 'In the morning, while it was still very dark, he got up and went out to a deserted place, and there he prayed.' (Mark 1:35). Indeed on this occasion Jesus found such a good place that Mark goes on to tell us how it took a while for the disciples to find him.

Luke also records how Jesus' popularity led to an increasing need for space: 'But now more than ever the word about Jesus spread abroad; many crowds would gather to hear him and to be cured of their diseases. But he would withdraw to deserted places and pray.' (Luke 5:15-16)

Luke also tells us how Jesus went off alone before choosing the twelve disciples and then giving the sermon on the plain: 'Jesus went out to the mountain to pray; and he spent the night in prayer to God.' (Luke 6:12)

Following the death of John the Baptist and after the feeding of the 5,000, and just before he walked on the waters of Lake Galilee, Jesus needed a break: 'He dismissed the crowds. And after he had dismissed the crowds, he went up the mountain by himself to pray. When evening came, he was there alone.' (Matt 14:22b-23 cf Mark 6:46)

There is no clear evidence that Jesus prayed with anyone else. The disciples are certainly nearby on occasions (see Luke 9:18 and most notably in the Garden at Gethsemane [Matthew 26:36ff and Mark 14:32ff]) and he certainly prayed for people: the disciples (John 17), Simon, in particular (Luke 22:32) and children (Matt 19:15-16), for example. One can also interpret other occasions as prayers: blessing people and bread, and his prayers from the Cross: 'Father, forgive them; for they do not know what they are doing.' (Luke 23:24)

If there is one thing we can learn from Jesus' own practice it is that he prayed before, during, and after events and encounters. Fundamentally, Jesus' stability through prayer was to be alone: just him and God.

What solitary times and places do you have?

In his humanity

In the normal day-to-day activities of life, it is clear Jesus valued the company of other people. The central group of twelve plus the female followers and disciples such as Mary Magdalene, Salome (thought by many to be the sister of Mary, the mother of Jesus), Joanna, Susanna, Lazarus, Mary and Martha and of course his own mother and siblings were all part of who Jesus was in his life on earth and his stability within it.

Jesus ate and drank. He cried and laughed. As a child, he would have played and sat on his mother's lap (although maybe not quite like many pictures would have us believe). He would have watched Joseph at work, learning the trade in the process. He travelled on land and sea. He slept inside and outdoors. Like anyone else, he experienced many of those stabilising factors which are part of the daily life of a lot of people.

And he also experienced times when his boat was being tossed about. He knew what it was to be let down and to be betrayed by others. He experienced pain: both emotionally and physically.

Yet, there is a lot we don't know about the fully human nature of Jesus. Many have speculated on different aspects, some of which raise questions which disturb our stability.

Let's for a moment return to the 12 year-old Jesus at the Temple. After searching for so long, Mary and Joseph found him and, as we saw, and subject to interpretation, they're weren't happy. Pope Francis once speculated, 'For this little "escapade", Jesus probably had to beg forgiveness of his parents. The Gospel doesn't say this, but I believe that we can presume it.'[lv] How do we react to the concept of Jesus saying sorry?

Or take another example, The Gospel of Philip (one of a number of non-canonical texts: in other words, writings not accepted as part of the New Testament) writes about Mary Magdalene and that Jesus 'loved her more than all the disciples and used to kiss her'.[lvi] Jesus was, as we have already observed, fully human, as well as fully divine, so could he not also have love for a woman? Might that lead us to ask other discomforting, destabilising questions – was Jesus disabled? Was he a person of colour? Was he gay? If not, does that mean that those who are are not fully human?

We will each have our own answers to those questions. Some will reply with a loud and emphatic 'No' to all. Some may have a view that if he was any of those, does it actually make any difference to the Jesus they believe in?

The author of Hebrews tells us that Jesus was 'like his brothers and sisters in every respect' (2:17) and that 'we do not have a high priest who is unable to sympathize with our weaknesses, but we have one who in every respect has been tested as we are, yet without sin' (4:15).

Cally Hammond observed how St Augustine 'Saw that once we are clear about the basic point that God is good, and made us good, that is enough reassurance to carry us through the difficult questions we don't understand.'[lvii]

Being asked difficult questions and asking difficult questions is, just like for the disciple Thomas, part of finding our places of stability.

What aspects of Jesus' humanity aid your stability?

In the Garden (Matt 26:36-56; Mark 14:32-52)

One only has to remember the sweat and tears shed by Jesus in the Garden at Gethsemane as he waited to be arrested and crucified to understand how challenging the worst of storms can be.

Jesus experienced the anxiety of waiting for what was to come. Jesus could have decided to run away from the Garden or to use his miraculous skills to escape from the soldiers. Or when Simon of Cyrene came to help carry the cross, Jesus could have left him with it and disappeared into the crowd... he could have avoided the storm.

How many of us have at some point echoed Jesus' words: 'Father, if you are willing, remove this cup from me' – and struggled to add, 'yet, not my will but yours be done.' (Luke 22:42)

In the Garden, he was met by his betrayer. And what does Jesus say to him? 'Friend.'. Here is he faced with the man he knows to have told the authorities where he was for 30 pieces of silver and he calls him 'Friend.' (Matt 26:50)

Yes, Judas had his fingers in the purse. Yes, he walked into the Garden at Gethsemane and handed over the Messiah. Yes, he had betrayed not just Jesus but that whole group who had gone through so much together in the previous three years. After all, he'd witnessed healings and miracles. He'd listened to the teaching. He'd walked and prayed. He was given the same authority to minister to others as the rest of the disciples. He'd had his feet washed. He received that first communion. Judas had become a friend. A close friend.

What love is this? Who then is this?

'Not my will but yours be done.'

The ultimate statement of trust?

The ultimate way of finding stability in times of change?

On the Cross

It doesn't end in the Garden of course. First, there is the trial – and the beatings – and the humiliation. Some of the time, Jesus says nothing. He stays silent amidst all that is happening around and to him. Other times he responds enigmatically. He causes Pontius Pilate to wrestle with his conscience. And, in a fashion that strikes us as all too familiar in modern-day leaders, the Roman governor essentially tries to avoid the problem in the hope that it will disappear. Like many of us at times, Pilate finds himself stuck 'between a rock and a hard place'. A dilemma. A situation where there is no easy answer or way forward. Some situations may ultimately lead us, like Pilate, to 'wash our hands' of it. To stick with what we personally believe. To maintain our own integrity. To say courageously with Pilate, 'what I have written I have written' (John 19:22). Jesus' trial raises questions for us about how we maintain stability in the worst of storms.

And if things couldn't get any worse... they did.

The Cross.

As he hung there, Jesus is recorded as speaking seven times. As you read through these now, take time to consider not only Jesus' own stability but also your own:

Forgiveness – 'Father, forgive them for they do not know what they do.' (Luke 23:34). What place does forgiveness – both for and of yourself and of and by other people hold in your sense of stability?

Salvation – 'Today you will be with me in paradise.' (Luke 23:43) In what ways does that promise support your sense of stability?

Relationship – 'Behold your son: behold your mother.' (John 19:26-27) What role do relationships with others help or hinder your sense of stability?

Abandonment – 'My God, my God, why have you forsaken me?' (Matthew 27:46) Carefully reflect on how your experience of such times affected how you felt.

Distress – 'I thirst.' (John 19:28) What did you learn from a time when you were thirsty for Christ?

Triumph – 'It is finished.' (John 19:30) How does the prospect of such a moment aid your sense of stability?

Reunion – 'Father, into your hands I commit my spirit.' (Luke 23:46) Spend some time dwelling on these words. Repeat them as a prayer.

In his divinity

Jesus endured a very human life and a horrific human death. Many have speculated about whether Jesus remained 'fully human' after his resurrection or whether he was a 'hybrid', to use an increasingly common noun, of both fully human and fully divine. His request to Mary Magdalene not to touch him on that morning of the Resurrection is sometimes interpreted in that way (John 20:17). We also have those occasions when Jesus simply 'appears' to the disciples in a room (John 20:19-23, 26-29; Luke 24:36-49) and to the two travellers on the road to Emmaus – and then disappears (Luke 24:13-32). Morwenna Ludlow observes, 'The experience of

Mary and the disciples on the way to Emmaus doesn't so much show that Jesus' composition has changed; rather the resurrection has changed their understanding of who Jesus is.'[lviii]

It may seem strange to consider Jesus' sense of finding stability through being fully divine. In many respects, one might be more comfortable with the Jesus who is fully divine rather than the Jesus who was fully human. The latter, as we have seen raises uncomfortable questions but it is through such questions, by finding our way through the rougher waters of belief that we are brought closer to the Jesus who is both fully divine and fully human. Luigi Gioia sums up the relevance of Jesus' life, death and resurrection for us as we negotiate the storms:

> 'The risen Christ can reach down to the deepest corners in which we are hiding and there he shows us his hands and his side. This is an important gesture. It is Jesus' way of saying to us: "I know what you are suffering because I shared it. I know your sadness because I felt it, I know your feeling of having been abandoned by God because I screamed it, I know your loneliness because I was betrayed by all my friends. But thanks to me all this suffering has become a source of life, light, peace, and joy, and it reopens the doors, it abolishes the walls, it restores the relationship with the Father."'[lix]

8. Feeling bruised

So how do these Lake Galilee-type life events affect us on a more personal level?

In thinking about that, you may like to bring to mind such an event in your own life. Doing so also helps in understanding that many of the reactions we have in such times are quite normal and natural, albeit uncomfortable and difficult.

Immediately after a major, perhaps traumatic, life event, it is common for people to feel shocked, numb, or unable to accept what has happened. In such times, we might feel 'cut off' from our feelings or from what is going on around us. We may have feelings of denial and can't accept that it has happened. Indeed, we may behave as though it hasn't and others are led to believe we are stronger than we actually feel. Over time these feelings of shock and denial gradually fade, and other thoughts and feelings take their place. We'll now explore some of these psychological reactions.[lx]

People react differently and take different amounts of time to come to terms with such events. Even so, like the disciples in the boat, we may be surprised by the strength of the storm and the power of those feelings. It is also very normal to experience a mix of emotions and reactions.

We may feel:

- **Frightened** that the same thing will happen again or that we might lose control of our feelings and break down.

- **Helpless**, vulnerable and overwhelmed.

- **Angry** about what has happened and with whoever was responsible.

- **Guilty** that we have survived when others have suffered or died and/or that we couldn't or didn't do something to prevent it.

- **Sad** particularly if people were injured or killed and especially if it's someone we knew.

- **Ashamed or embarrassed** that we have strong feelings we can't control, especially if we need others to support us.

- **Relieved** that the danger is over.

- **Hopeful** that life will return to normal. People can start to feel more positive about things quite soon after a trauma.

Strong feelings such as those can affect our physical health too. In the weeks or months afterwards we may be unable to sleep, feel very tired, dream a lot and have nightmares; have poor concentration, memory problems, and have difficulty thinking clearly; physically, we might suffer from headaches or other aches and pains; experience changes in appetite, sex-drive or libido; or feel that our heart is beating faster.

It may take time to accept what has happened and to learn to live with the impact. Time may be needed to grieve for what or who has been lost. At such times it's important to do some things and not to do others...

- **Be honest about feelings**. Strong feelings are natural. Don't feel embarrassed about them. Bottling them up can make us feel worse and can damage our health. Bit by bit, think about the trauma and talk about it with others. Don't worry about crying, it's natural and usually helpful. Take things at a pace that you feel comfortable with.

- **Being and doing**. Being active can take the mind off what has happened, but time is also needed to go over it all to help come to terms with it. Take some time to get back to your old routine. Even if you don't feel much like eating, try to have regular meals and to eat a balanced diet. Taking some exercise can help – but start gently. Do some 'normal' things with other people – sometimes we will want to be with other people, but not to talk about what has happened. This can also be part of the healing process.

- **Don't drink or use drugs**. Excess alcohol or drugs can blot out painful memories for a while, but they will stop the process of coming to terms with what has happened. They can also cause depression and other health problems and potentially alienate those who want to help.

- **Don't make any major life changes**. Try to put off any big decisions. Our judgment may not be at its best and choices may be made which are later regretted.

- **Take care**. After a trauma, people are more likely to have accidents. For example, be careful around the home and when driving.

If mental or physical wellbeing is giving cause for concern then do seek professional help through a GP or counsellor. Talk early, don't let it get worse and that will help in finding a better, calmer place after the storm.[lxi]

A lot of people talk about PTSD – Post-Traumatic Stress Disorder. Like a number of mental health-related terms – such as 'They're a little bit OCD' or 'I'm having a panic attack' – the term PTSD is sometimes used quite flippantly and totally dismisses the real impact of such conditions. PTSD can develop immediately after someone experiences a disturbing event, or it can occur weeks, months or even years later. PTSD is estimated to affect about 1 in every 3 people who have a traumatic experience, but it's not clear exactly why some people develop the condition and others do not.[lxii]

As with all medical conditions, don't 'Dr Google' them – go to where the evidence-based information is such as the NHS website[lxiii] or a recognised mental health charity[lxiv] or talk to a qualified health professional.

Rough seas

Let's now turn to other aspects of stormy weather – maybe not as traumatic but nonetheless difficult to handle. As mentioned before, attitudes towards mental illness have improved considerably - in particular over the last two decades. But there are still difficulties for those who experience mental ill health, not least, alas, in some areas of the church. 'It has...been the experience of many sufferers that the implicit message in church is that depression is "laziness", anxiety is a "lack of trust" and that mental health problems can be resolved by greater "obedience to Christ",' observes Will Van Der Hart, a director of The Mind and Soul Foundation.[lxv] 'Depression, anxiety, and mental anguish are not signs you are a bad Christian,' adds Jo Swinney.[lxvi]

Feeling anxious or depressed at certain times is perfectly normal. We're bound to feel anxious if we're facing an important exam or a relative is in hospital, for example. It's natural to feel down or low, say, after a bereavement or the break up of a relationship. Indeed, those emotions and responses are a necessary part of who we are as human beings – and integral to our ability to cope with difficult situations.

But it is right to be concerned when those feelings or symptoms affect our ability to function. When work, sleep, family life and other everyday matters are increasingly affected, help needs to be sought. In many cases, family and friends will probably be able to see you through a difficult time. However, it may be necessary to seek professional help if the feelings are too much or go on for too long. As a general guide, if someone is experiencing feelings of depression or anxiety most of the day, every day for a fortnight then that's the time to go to the doctor – talk early, and don't let it get worse.

The difficulty is that a lot of people don't seek help that quickly. We feel we 'ought' or 'should' be able to cope. We might tell ourselves 'not to be so stupid'. Others might tell us to 'pull ourselves together'. Talk early, don't let it get worse.

Asking for help is not a sign of failure. We are called to 'bear one another's burdens' (Galatians 6:2) so it is important to let others bear ours at times. Paradoxically, although not unusually, the act, or even the very thought, of seeking help may feel frightening at first. We may be scared of 'what will come out' or worried about 'what's wrong' or concerned about what other people will think (especially in some church circles, sadly).

Asking for help is a sign of strength. But it is important to be realistic. If things have become difficult, it may get tougher before it gets easier. It's easy to slip into a pattern of negative thinking – and it takes time to change one's default thought patterns. Cognitive Behavioural Therapy (CBT) can be helpful with this. CBT is based on the concept that our thoughts, feelings, physical sensations and actions are interconnected, and that negative thoughts and feelings can trap us in a vicious cycle of thoughts and behaviour. CBT aims to help change these negative thought patterns to improve the way we feel.[lxvii] It's been shown to be particularly helpful for people experiencing mild to moderate levels of anxiety and depression. Medication may help but isn't always necessary. However, it will take time and effort – which is in itself part of the reason why so many people end up struggling for so long: simply because it takes so much time and so much effort.

When the storm is rocking our boat, David Adam encourages us to not let Jesus sleep in our lives. 'We struggle on alone and are often overwhelmed because we do not call upon him in the storm... In the storms of fear and sorrow, when we are feeling overwhelmed, we need to know the presence and the power of our God. We need to know again that God can bring order out of chaos and that Christ can give us his peace.'[lxviii]

Sailing in calmer waters

The good news is that people experiencing a period of anxiety and/or depression do get better. Unlike many physical health conditions, recovery from a period of mental ill health may not mean the complete absence of symptoms but it will see the return to a more comfortable level of day-to-day functioning.

Here are some suggestions to help remain sailing in calmer waters (and the rougher ones when they reoccur):

- **Every day**. It can be helpful to think about what can be done that is beneficial. Like going for a walk, reading a book (if concentration allows – maybe make sure it's an easy, light read), listening to music, gardening, painting, baking – whatever fills your soul. Write those things down so they can be an easily accessible reminder when it's tough to know what to do. Some people find exercise helpful. If possible, get out of the home at least once a day. One Twitter user I've come across takes a cup of tea when going for a walk each day to help her mental well-being.[lxix] Think also about other occasional beneficial things to fill the soul – going to the theatre or visiting particular places and meeting people who are special to us.

- **Night time** is often difficult. Try and decide before going to bed what to think about when lying awake. Make a list (and keep it on the bedside table as a reminder). A list of neutral things such as an enjoyable holiday, a film, a book, a hymn. Before going to bed write a separate list of worries and anxieties (not to be kept on the bedside table): they can wait until the morning – honestly, they can.

- **Habits**. Contrary to what many people think and believe, it is possible to 'change a habit of a lifetime'. Yes, it will take a lot of conscious effort – it's reckoned one has to do something or think in a different way all day, every day for several weeks for our habits to change. Some of the most difficult are our 'thinking habits' but even they can be changed if we really want to have a more healthy and beneficial effect.

- **Triggers**. Try to recognise what triggers, what causes or initiates, difficult thoughts and feelings. What could be done to handle those triggers more helpfully? Think about what might be called 'default settings' – for example, if something difficult happens, is the immediate reaction to panic or to get angry? If someone is trying to help, is the response one of trying to find a way of disagreeing with them or giving reasons why it won't work? Is our default answer 'No' or 'Yes'?

Thinking about how we react and whether those reactions are helpful or unhelpful can be beneficial. (CBT can help rethink our thinking in that respect also.)

- **Patterns**. Getting to know our own particular pattern of moods can be helpful: for example, feeling tired will often result in feeling low so it's important to know that it's OK and natural to be tired (especially if sleep is also affected). Do we find we feel a particular way at a particular time of day? If so, it's helpful to acknowledge that fact and how it changes as the day goes on. If something is helping, do it. If something doesn't help, try and stop it from happening.

- **Give yourself time**. It takes time to change. The process of transition takes its course and while uncomfortable at times, it is important to be kind to yourself as it takes place. It can also be helpful to understand what is happening while change takes place, particularly when starting something new. Often attributed to the American psychologist, Abraham Maslow (he of the 'Hierarchy of Needs' theory, if you've ever come across that), when we learn new things we progress through 'Four Stages of Competence':[lxx]

  - **Stage 1** – Unconscious incompetence – "I don't know what I don't know."

  - **Stage 2** – Conscious incompetence – "I have no idea what this all means or how to do it."

- **Stage 3** – Conscious competence – "Some of this is beginning to make sense – and I can actually do bits of it!"

- **Stage 4** – Unconscious competence – "I've learned what to do and I can do it 'without thinking about it'."

These can equally be applied to other situations involving change and it's helpful to recognise which stage we are in and how we move from one to another (sometimes without realising it).

- **Progress**. When looking after ourselves it can be helpful to try and think of it as being like the financial markets – the value goes up and down but the general trend is always up. Having 'touch points' to reflect on can be helpful in noticing our progress. Many people have a tendency only to think about bigger issues and be left feeling they haven't progressed very much. It can be helpful to think back to the last time a similar event happened (whether it was simple or complex) or to recognise those occasions when 'I couldn't have done that a month/year ago...' Progress can be and is often best measured in very small ways.

- **Feeling happy**. When experiencing a period of depression or anxiety, don't feel guilty in those times when feeling happier or more relaxed (it's surprising how many people do). It's OK to have good thoughts about oneself. 'Dealing with emotional pain is not self-indulgent, any more than dealing with physical pain is,' Will Van Der Hart once wrote.[lxxi]

Jesus said: 'You shall love your neighbour as yourself,' (Mark 12:31). Probably most of us feel comfortable with the 'love your neighbour' bit... thinking of others, being kind to people... 'Yep, I can do that. That bit's OK.'

But what about, 'as yourself'? To love ourselves in the same way as we love others.

Umm... more tricky that.

Many of us focus on our failings. The bad bits. The mistakes. The wrong words. The difficult memories. The hurts. The things we messed up.

There are good things in all of us. It may be hard to focus on them at times, but they're there. The things we got right. The successes (they don't have to be showstoppers). The compliments we receive (even if we struggle to actually believe them). What we're good at. What we like about ourselves.

Loving ourselves requires having a balanced view of who we are. Having a balanced view enables us to see what God, in his love and grace, has made good within us.

God's love isn't based on success and achievement. You don't have to prove anything. God loves you no less than anyone else (complete with all the good bits and all the bits we don't like that much).

What do you love about yourself?

Maybe ask yourself these questions – and write down the responses as a reminder to yourself:

- What am I like when I am well and happy?

- What do I do that keeps me well and happy?

- What do I notice when I'm beginning to struggle? (and is that because I'm not doing that which keeps me well and happy?)

9. Sailing on

For all they encountered on that stormy crossing of Lake Galilee, at least the disciples knew what to do. Jesus was in the boat with them and they asked him for help. They asked him to restore their stability.

The message is clear. Life gets stormy but Jesus is in the boat with us, in the midst of the storm, and we can ask him for help.

And... you've probably heard that more times than the disciples crossed the lake.

But how easy it is to forget. How easy it is to panic and to shout. How easy it is to lose our sense of faith and trust in such circumstances. How easy it is to lose stability in times of change.

'In a storm,' writes Mark Bradford, 'there's a force of things happening around us, and being done to us, that we cannot control. Yet Jesus has been there and he models a way to be faithful to the Father, under massive, even overwhelming, pressure.'[lxxii] In the midst of the storm, in the midst of their fear, in the midst of their lack of faith, they asked our Lord for help – and then, as Beverly

Zink-Sawyer put it, 'The disciples are rendered speechless in the face of Jesus' great work. They respond with awe and with a glimmer of understanding of the nature and power of Jesus.'[lxxiii]

So far, we've considered different types of storms, the various life events that happen around and to us and how they impact our wellbeing and general ability to function. We've thought about some of our responses to those difficult occasions and the ways that we look after our mental wellbeing in particular. We've reflected on the experience of other people and how they found stability in times of change.

In this final section, we turn specifically to considering some very practical ways of finding and maintaining stability in times of change. And how through doing so we encounter the unchanging nature of God and how that reveals the presence of Jesus in our life's boat.

Read & Pray

Christopher Jamison describes prayer as 'a simple act of addressing God as "you"…To pray is to address God as a familiar friend – to speak to "you" rather than to think about "Him".'[lxxiv]

And yet, and yet, we have made it, oh, so complicated…

… and yet, there is no one, single, right way to pray or to read the Bible.

The reason why many of us find reading and praying so difficult is perhaps because we are trying to be like someone else. We try to be a better Christian based on what we think other people do. 'I wish I could pray like you', 'I should be reading the Bible every day like you but...'

If we continue to try to be like someone else then we will always have a sense of failure and inadequacy. As Cally Hammond put it, 'It is a mistake... to compare the outside of other people's lives with the inside of our own life.'[lxxv] Or as Oscar Wilde is reputed to have said, 'Be yourself – because everyone else is taken.'

In times of change, it can be very difficult to pray and read the Bible. We perhaps don't know how to or what words to use in prayer. We might sit in silence hoping God will speak and nothing seems to happen. We might open the Bible hoping to read a spot-on verse. And of course, you'd expect me to say that stability is found by praying and by reading the Bible. But I'm not advocating the simplistic, storm-avoiding Gospel according to Nemo – 'Just keep praying, just keep praying...' In the same way that we have to face the storms, it's important to be realistic and honest in our prayers and the difficulties we may encounter within them and in our reading of scripture.

Finding ways of prayer and reading the Bible that suits you as you are, the person God made you to be, and also suits your relationship with God are crucial to finding stability in times of change.

God wants you to be you.

There are many, many different approaches to personal times of prayer and Bible reading and some are shown below. But these are simply keys to unlocking all that God has for you – they are a means to an end, not the end itself.

- **Centering Prayer**. In The Cloud of Unknowing, written by an anonymous 14th century English monk, the author describes how to keep oneself focused when distractions come by centering our attention on a word or phrase: 'Choose a short word. Fix it in your mind so that it will remain there come what may,' he writes. 'Should some thought go on annoying you, answer with this one word alone. Let this little word represent to you God in all his fullness and nothing less than the fullness of God. Let nothing except God hold sway in your mind and heart.'[lxxvi] This ancient method of contemplative prayer has been revived in our time as 'Centering Prayer' and made popular by people such as Thomas Keating and Marina Widerkehr.

- **Daily reading**. There are numerous versions of this approach to a regular quiet time. Organisations such as BRF, Bible Society, Scripture Union (SU), United Christian Broadcasters (UCB) and Waverley Abbey Resources (CWR) and others provide printed 'daily notes' and there are numerous apps and other sources which are good for providing structure and discipline. But don't feel guilty if you miss a day – as we all know, storms happen.

- **Online resources and apps** such as Sacred Space, Pray as you Go and Common Worship Daily Prayer are other helpful resources for a daily rhythm. Times to sit at your computer or device and pray. A cautionary note, though – technology is very good at causing distractions so closing down email and other programmes and apps helps in paying intentional attention to God.

- **Icons and other images**. Many of us were taught to close our eyes when we pray. Praying with icons is an ancient prayer practice that involves keeping our eyes wide open, taking into our heart what the image visually communicates. We focus not on what is seen in the icon or other sacred paintings or images, but rather on what is seen through it. Icons have been described as windows on prayer.

- **Lectio Divina (holy reading)** is not Bible study but is about pondering on the word to enable prayer. Continuing his earlier theme, Christopher Jamison writes, 'Just as prayer involves a person speaking to God as "you", so Lectio Divina involves God speaking to the reader as "you".'[lxxvii] Stages comprise reading a very short Bible passage two or three times (lectio); then meditation, taking a word or phrase that strikes you and ruminating upon it (meditatio); leading into prayer, open, honest conversation with God (oratio); and then resting in God, the silent prayer of contemplation (contemplatio). **Visio Divina (holy seeing)** takes a similar approach as Lectio but using images such as paintings, icons or photographs.

- **Spiritual Exercises of St Ignatius of Loyola** are best done with the accompaniment of a spiritual director or via a guided retreat – as encountered in full they are not for the faint-hearted. 'The goal is not to reach the end of the exercises but to experience God in the midst of them,' wrote Larry Warner.[lxxviii] However, on a simpler note, Ignatius encourages the use of the scriptures imaginatively to encounter God and to grow as a more Christ-like person. For example, you may like to imagine that you are on that boat on Lake Galilee and pray through what it was like both in the storm and in the calm.

- **The Prayer of Examen (Examen of Consciousness)** is also accredited to Ignatius of Loyola. At the heart of this approach is an increasing awareness of God's presence and the Holy Spirit's movement throughout the day. The Examen is primarily an exercise in remembering. One is invited, through four portions (presence, gratitude, review and response), to concentrate on experiences and encounters from the past day. The beauty of the practice is its simplicity; it is more of a guide than a prescription. If some portion feels especially important on a given day, feel the freedom to spend all or most of your time in that portion. The purpose is to increase awareness and sensitivity, not to finish or accomplish a task.

- **Time & Place**. Setting aside such periods to give intentional attention to God is an important element in our striving for stability and is about enabling such encounters to become part of the natural rhythm of the day or the week. As natural as the time you set aside for getting dressed or having a meal. It just becomes part of the daily routine. Alongside setting aside the time, setting aside the place is also helpful. For Jesus, it was the mountains and other places where he could be alone. Having a specific place within one's home can help: a place set apart for prayer, Bible study, worship, or whichever way enables you to deepen your relationship with God. A place free from other distractions. A place set aside for you and God to meet.

- **Your own approach** – as mentioned above, a key aspect of finding stability in times of change is to find an approach to prayer and reading the Bible and other aspects of your faith and experience of God that reflect both you and your relationship with God. What other people do is of no consequence (apart from negatively). If someone else finds daily Bible reading notes helpful then that's great but it may not suit you. If someone doesn't find structured liturgical prayers helpful that doesn't mean to say that you won't. What suits you as the person you are?

Whichever 'method(s)' you choose, the key thing is giving intentional attention to God. All that said, isn't it wonderful that we can give intentional attention to God at any time, day or night, any place, anywhere and that too is something to nurture and practise.

When Jesus is asleep

Even when we feel we are using all the 'right methods' (even if we accept there is no one single 'right' way) there can be times when Jesus seems to be asleep, when God feels absent.

'My God, my God, why have you abandoned me?' Those haunting words cried out by Jesus as he hung from the cross reflect a common human experience. Often within the storms of life we find two unanswered questions, 'Where are you, God?' and 'Why has this happened?'.

For centuries, indeed, millennia, people have asked questions about God's presence and absence. Where were you, God at Hillsborough or when Grenfell Tower burned? Where are you in Ukraine or the famines of the Horn of Africa? Why did you allow my mum to die when I was just 17? Why, when something seemed so right, did it go so wrong?

The Psalms, that great collection of words about the human condition, pull no punches on this topic... 'How long, O Lord? Will you forget me forever? How long will you hide your face from me?' (Psalm13:1) 'O Lord, why do you cast me off?' (Psalm 88:14a)

As Christians, we often speak of having a relationship with God. In many ways, that relationship may well contain the same elements we find in those we have with people: anger, abandonment, disappointment, frustration, shouting and unanswered questions. That relationship also understands there are times when we need to express such emotions towards God.

Beth LaNeel Tanner put it like this, 'The personal cries of pain and brash accusations against God are not thoughts to be hidden from the throne of God but to be deposited with all their jagged edges and sharp cries before the face of God.'[lxxix]

In our relationships and friendships with others, we can also grow apart. It is one of my deepest sadnesses that I have lost contact with so many friends over the years – people I thought I meant something to. But a lot of that was down to me not keeping in touch as well. So it is with God. If we don't 'keep in touch' – not just through prayer but also actively looking for God's presence in our lives – then we may well grow apart from God. As a vicar I once knew used to say, 'If God seems far away – who's moved?'.

If God seems far away or feels absent then it's important to consider what we're doing to 'find' (or to 'distance') God. For unlike human relationships, where both presence and absence occur, God is, ultimately, never absent.

But neither can we just sit back and wait for God to make that presence known. In a prayer, Frank Skinner offers another slant on this very human aspect of our God-focused relationship: 'You seem a long way away tonight. Maybe it's me. Maybe I don't want you to hear me too clearly.'[lxxx]

The more we look for God's presence, the more we will see God present and the more God will show us that presence.

Listening for God

The very first word in the Rule of St Benedict is the word, 'Listen.'[lxxxi] Listen is an anagram of 'silent'. Listening requires silence and silence enables us to listen. American nun and author, Joan Chittister writes, 'Silence is a cornerstone of Benedictine life and spiritual development. The Rule does not call for absolute silence; it calls for thoughtful talk.'lxxxii

The word listen comes from the word obedience. Pope Francis describes the meaning very clearly: 'The word "obey" comes from Latin, it means to listen, to hear others. Obeying God is listening to God, and having an open heart to follow the path that God points out to us. Obedience to God is listening to God and it sets us free.'lxxxiii

Listening to God amidst all the noise of our surroundings and the constant chattering of our mind takes practice. God doesn't speak on command but often when we are not expecting it.

Of all the voices going on in our head, to be able to identify that which is God's is helpful. For some, it may sound very slightly different: a different tone, pitch or phrasing of words. Perhaps coming from thoughts that have not been our own. All the same, how do we know it is actually God speaking?

We might sense deep down inside that actually no, that isn't God – it's us (or other people) wanting it to be. Equally, we might recognise God speaking through events that happen. Or that holy nudge which led us to visit someone or to pray for someone and we find out that it was God. God doesn't just use words to speak to us. Circumstances, actions by others or ourselves, dreams... many, many ways. For this is God and God knows no bounds (only ours).

Sometimes the listening takes place over a period of time. Maybe days, weeks, months, perhaps even years. We sit with what we think God may be saying and we wait to see if those thoughts remain. To wait and see if they are confirmed by others; or by the practicalities of following through with what we think God might be saying; or by what the Bible or other words that come to our attention confirm or not.

This is about listening to and for God. About giving God intentional attention.

We are, as St Benedict puts it, to 'listen with the ear of our heart.'[lxxxiv]

The sound of silence

A few years ago, I had some hearing tests. I had a sense that perhaps something wasn't quite right – particularly if there was a lot of background noise. I was referred to the hospital and they did a range of tests all of which were perfectly normal. I sat with the consultant. 'You appear to have an obscure auditory dysfunction,' he said. 'So, you mean you don't know what it is?' I replied. 'Correct,' he said magnanimously. 'What you need to do is to focus your hearing.'

So in the same way that many of us wear glasses to focus on what we are seeing, so too do we need to focus our hearing.

Such listening often requires silence. But silence is often difficult. If there's a gap in the conversation, we can feel compelled to fill it rather than experience the awkwardness or embarrassment of what to say next. The ability to be silent with others – and to be allowed to be silent – can often be a true mark of how comfortable we are in someone's company. If being silent with other people is difficult then how much more it can be with God. Or at least it can seem that way.

It is, at times, undoubtedly difficult to discern what God is saying to us – and how often we complete God's sentences in the process. It's very easy to decide what God is saying.

God does use words and also actions, events and circumstances to speak to us but as St John of the Cross put it, 'God's first language is silence.'[lxxxv] Commenting on this beautiful, rich insight the aforementioned Thomas Keating, wrote: 'Everything else is a poor translation. In order to understand this language, we must learn to be silent and to rest in God.'[lxxxvi]

Barbara Brown Taylor writes 'Our words are too fragile. God's silence is too deep. Silence is as much a sign of God's presence as of God's absence, divine silence is not a vacuum to be filled but a mystery to be entered into.'[lxxxvii]

Silence frees us from some of the distractions of everyday life and allows us to listen and to give intentional attention to God.

And yet, being silent doesn't automatically mean that God will speak. It's easy to think, 'Right, your turn now, God. I'm going to sit here for ten minutes in silence and I expect to hear from you!'

So we sit in silence, wanting to hear God's voice, just like Samuel: 'Speak, Lord, for your servant is listening' (1 Samuel 3:10). And we may well hear it in such times but God also 'speaks through the earthquake, wind and fire'.[lxxxviii] Speaks through the noise that surrounds us. Speaks at times when we are not expecting it. Speaks in the storm.

'If you find yourself in silence at some point today, take a moment to listen to it,' writes Amy Scott-Robinson. 'The God who is silence does not answer all our questions. He does not instantly solve all our problems or change our direction to something new and exciting. He does not come as we're expecting. He does not give us what we're looking for. He gives us what we need.'[lxxxix]

David Walker takes this practical impact of silence before God further: 'I know that when I have drawn close to God, in silence and stillness, or in opening up the pain and desire of my heart to him, I feel different inwardly. I might not notice how it is doing so, but I would bet that such a feeling has an impact on how I treat the people around me, how I handle my daily tasks, and even how I feel about myself.'[xc]

Distractions, distractions, distractions

If you are not used to long periods of silence in prayer or meditation, you may like to bear in mind some of the following which often causes the 'background noise' and affects our ability to focus hearing.

- **Distracting thoughts are normal** – in times of silence, and in prayer in general for that matter, we find ourselves thinking about other things (people, work, domestic tasks, TV, etc). Don't worry about having these thoughts but try to put them to one side and draw your mind back to your prayer and meditation by...

- Having something to look at (e.g. a candle or an icon).

- Using a verse from the Bible or a simple prayer such as 'Jesus, remember me when I come into your kingdom' or a word like 'Maranatha' ('Come, Lord'). Simply repeat the words.

- Imagining the thought is like a leaf floating on a river & passing you by – just let it go past (don't jump in and grab it!).

- Say 'Hello' to the thought and then say 'See you later'.

- **Write down** anything you think may be from God. Many people find keeping a journal helpful: a place to record insights, thoughts, reflections, or words. Something to go back to at a later time also. Doing so can also help in discerning the way forward – seeing how those thoughts may (or may not) have developed and changed as time goes by.

- **Holding something**. Some people find using a Rosary or a Holding Cross or a similar physical item helps focus our hearing. Frank Skinner reflected on this in what he calls his 'freeform chats': 'The Rosary is a tighter structure, so I guess that will operate like a supporting rhythm, while these prayers are the like the improvised solo: some bum notes but some exhilarating discoveries.'[xci]

- **Don't worry if you fall asleep**. That may simply be an indication of how much you need some rest. While we might feel embarrassed if we fall asleep in the company of others, God has a history of speaking to people through dreams so you never know what might happen!

- **Don't force yourself to be holy**. As the 17th century monk, Brother Lawrence wrote in response to a letter he had received: 'She seems to me full of goodwill, but she would go faster than grace. One does not become holy all at once.'[xcii] Or as Thomas Merton put it, 'Don't seek self-indulgent serenity.'[xciii] So, don't worry if 'nothing happens'.

Longer periods of silence such as that found on a quiet day or on retreat can also be helpful. But, if the use of silence is new for you or unsettling (or if you live alone, a constant and rather uncomfortable companion) be cautious about approaches which advocate diving straight in for 20 minutes or several days. Build up gradually: take it slowly. Aim for two minutes a day to begin with. Maybe go for five the next week. If silence doesn't suit you: that's fine. If silence becomes your friend then just like spending time with other people, you may find that it will gradually lengthen without realising it. Remember, there is no pass mark.

A space for words

Between the silence, there is often a space for words. Spoken prayer, whether the liturgy or 'set prayers' that have been used over the centuries or our own extemporary prayers provide such a valuable and important way of communicating with God. They allow us to freely praise God for his marvellous goodness and blessing. Other times, we might echo the words of the disciples in the boat: Lord, don't you care that I'm perishing? Quite often – indeed a lot of the time – our prayers will simply comprise a list of requests for other people and for ourselves.

In the same way that we might find silence difficult, some find it hard to pray aloud: particularly in the company of other people. We might feel self-conscious or think we have to say 'the right thing' or use 'the right words'. It's also remarkably easy to end up listening to someone's words and phrases rather than praying with them: 'Well, I'm not going to say amen to that...' We may even be tempted to use prayers as a way of conveying a specific point about someone or an issue (as if God didn't already know about it...). We might even find ourselves playing 'prayer bingo': counting how many times the intercessor says the word 'Lord...'. Prayer is to be the sentence not the punctuation.

Cally Hammond writes 'We are not to sit around debating what to put in front of God so that he can select out whatever he decides to say "yes" to. Instead, we are to take our needs to him even though they may be trivial and insignificant, because at that moment, trivial or not, that is where we are, and they are what is on our mind. And that is all that matters.'[xciv] John Cassian, who lived c360-435 wrote 'Wherefore, we ought to pray often but briefly, lest if we are long about it our crafty foe may succeed in implanting something in our heart.'[xcv]

In response to another question by the disciples, Jesus himself taught us how to pray by giving us the Lord's Prayer (Matt 6:9-13;

Luke 11:2b-4). He also talked about the act of praying itself: 'And whenever you pray, do not be like the hypocrites; for they love to stand and pray in the synagogues and at the street corners, so that they may be seen by others... But whenever you pray, go into your room and shut the door and pray to your Father who is in secret; and your Father who sees in secret will reward you.' (Matt 5:5-6)

Alongside this is an instruction to pray alone, an approach which echoes his own practice, the importance of praying with others is not discouraged.

Tim Barnett wrote:

> 'The early Christians were devoted to prayer. It was the driving force behind all that they did. Immediately following Jesus' ascension into Heaven, the eleven disciples returned to the upper room in Jerusalem. Luke records that the first activity of the disciples was to join together "devoting themselves to prayer" (Acts 1:14). From the very beginning of the early church, prayer has been primary... At the end of Peter's famous sermon at Pentecost, there is a similar act of devotion to prayer by the new believers. Acts 2:42 records, "And they devoted themselves to the apostles' teaching and the fellowship, to the breaking of bread and the prayers" (emphasis added). The church had just grown from a little over 100 people to about 3000 people, and their first response was devotion to prayer. The disciple's devotion to prayer was both ongoing and central.'[xcvi]

Praying with others, whether in silence or spoken, remains an important way of maintaining our stability in the faith: especially at times when we are finding it hard to pray. Mark Bradford sums this topic up well when he wrote about how he is reminded of 'the importance of both formality and informality in our devotions, of both set prayer and extempore prayer. The freedom of the latter is a wonderful gift that I have always appreciated. Yet I notice that in the toughest of times in my life, when my own words run out, I need to draw from the deposit of set words that have been honed and crafted through the ages, as well as to embrace the gift of silence.'[xcvii]

Being with other people

When my wife and I were going through a particularly difficult time, someone said to us: 'Don't worry if you can't pray because that's what the church is for.' The knowledge that other people are praying for us in times of change or times of difficulty is in itself a source of stability. But other people can also disrupt our stability. There can be times when we want to be alone and times when we want to be with other people – for a whole variety of reasons on both counts.

Reflecting on how the disciples fell asleep in the Garden at Gethsemane and subsequently deserted Jesus in all the trauma that was taking place, Mark Bradford recognises something within himself: 'When the weight of life bears down, my instinct can be to switch off my connection with those around me, even with God. I retreat into my own bubble, where I try to ignore everything. It's a self-preservation device, yet it not only fails to deal with the storm that rages, it also neglects my responsibility to those around me and, most vitally, causes me to lose my connection with Jesus.'[xcviii]

One of the greatest impacts of the storm called Covid was its effect on our ability to be with other people. Many died without the presence of their nearest and dearest. Grandparents and grandchildren could not meet. The health of care home residents deteriorated as they sat unvisited. Many shielded, never leaving their home for months on end. Social and sports clubs closed. People worked in their houses and home-schooled their children. Those who were already unemployed lost any routine and occupation provided by voluntary work and other activities. Churches closed. The isolated were isolated.

Lockdown easings brought freedom and joy for many – and anxiety and continued restrictions for others. 'The virus has robbed us of many things. It continues to rob us of any certainty,' as the BBC's Chris Mason put it at one point.[xcix]

But within it all, we also saw the best (and at some points the worst) of humanity. Neighbours helping neighbours. Key workers giving their all. People socially distanced: giving way on pavements like cars on a country lane. Face coverings provided a sense of mutual respect and safety. The hope brought by the expertise behind and the roll-out of the vaccination programme. Even Zoom did its bit to keep us talking. The absence of physical church perhaps also increased our dependence on and our faith and trust in God.

While many of us, myself included, are natural isolates, the pandemic period showed us just how vital being with or in contact with other people is to our personal stability. You can be a Christian without going to church – but it helps. It's good to have other people in the boat when there's a storm blowing.

Routine, routine, routine

In his Rule, St Benedict writes a lot about what we might think of as the rather mundane aspects of life which are part of our stability – such as sleep. Think how much better, how much more stable we feel when we are sleeping well. He also writes about meals and the amount people should drink. Not only can we not live without them but the very nature and routine of eating and drinking are an integral part of our health, wellbeing and stability. By contrast, where that provision is lacking, so stability reduces – we see that in society and the increased need for Foodbanks, for example. Or just think of ourselves and how grumpy we become when we haven't eaten.

As we have already acknowledged, having routines for the spiritual aspects are valuable and some of these may date back years, as a couple of other personal contributors to this book observed: 'At the time my two children were small I attended a Lent Course arranged at St Stephen's, Rochester Row run by Revd Freddie Temple,' wrote Celia as she thought back to the 1960s. 'As I was not at the time attending church though I had been confirmed when at school I asked him after his lecture what to do about religion for my children. He quoted "Knock and it shall be answered." So, I followed this and found I was back home in the church again. I am a cheerful person by temperament which, together with my faith, helps a lot to keep going amid the difficulties of not only the situation with Covid but with life in general as time goes by.'[c]

Covid times have also brought to the fore the value of having to change routines too. Brother Bernard, a member of the Order of Cistercians writes: 'Whereas pre-pandemic, our community's full membership met three times a year for four days in a convent for our Chapter meetings since lockdown we have been able to meet at least once a week via Zoom. We pray one of our five offices, read a chapter from the Rule of St Benedict, listen to a reflection on this, and study, discuss community matters, and/or simply socialise.'[ci]

Such times bring about new opportunities as a Team Vicar, Revd John Rosedale, observes: 'In 2020 when lockdown started, the rhythm of life was stopped at so many levels. Prayer meetings, church services, and social gatherings. With the encouragement of one person, I started a nightly Zoom Service for one of my churches which prior to Covid had two weekly prayer meetings. We'd never had Compline before but I chose it to give some structure. We have met every night except Christmas Eve/Day and New Year's Eve. We begin with Compline and then go into intercessions. From a weekly congregation of 60, we have an evening attendance between 10 and 20... The 'church' has never had so much prayer and it has carried me through difficult days regularly meeting members of this congregation.'[cii]

The value of such day-to-day activities and routines, whether that is in the practicalities of life or the spiritual elements, can't be underestimated. Indeed, routine is most often noticed when it's absent. The loss of normal routine activities like we all experienced in the pandemic, for example. Loss of routine often leads to loss of confidence and contact with others. It leads to a loss of stability. Maintaining some aspects of routine helps us to hold on to that which does not change and contributes to our sense of stability.

Thankfulness & Trust

Cultivating an increased sense of thankfulness also increases our sense of stability. Thanking God for every aspect of every day. Whether that is 'Thank you, God, for safe travel', 'Thank you, God, for that person', 'Thank you, God, for that phone call or text', 'Thank you, God, for the sunset', 'Thank you, God, for that car parking space'... Consciously thanking God for all we are given increases our awareness of God's presence in our lives and helps us understand what he wants for us as we wander through it. Using something like the Examen can be helpful in this or at the end of each day simply writing down all the ways we have seen God's presence in our lives.

Our stability is also improved by nurturing an increased sense of trust. I expect you've heard people say: 'Oh, just trust God and everything will be fine!' Yeah... Right... And does anyone ever tell us how to actually do it? No... not really.

We talk about the wisdom of hindsight – when it comes to trusting God it's sometimes about having the wisdom of hindsight in advance. What did we learn from God the last time something like this happened? What did God show us about himself in previous experiences? What can I put in place or be thinking to help navigate this particular storm?

As alluded to before, at least the disciples in the storm-tossed boat knew from their previous experience of being with him that Jesus would help them. They trusted him even if it was from 'little faith'.

Writing in the context of Covid, Steven Croft offers advice which applies to any difficult times of change: 'Have the courage in this time to go deeper into God and deeper into your faith and draw on the great reservoirs of courage God gives to his people in these seasons.'[ciii]

Verbalising our trust also helps: for example, starting each day by saying words from Psalm 25, 'To you, O Lord, I lift up my soul; Oh my God, in you I trust'. Simple words to say at any other time too – maybe ahead of a difficult meeting or situation or any other time when you need the reassurance of God's presence as you wander on. Something to give you a sense of stability.

Bringing together the interconnectedness of prayer and trust, Luigi Giola writes:

> 'Prayer is all about trust in God, a trust full of hope and desire, a loving trust. Prayer is all about entrusting ourselves, our lives and our cause to the Father. The depth of our prayer depends on the depth of our trust in God; our ability to persevere in prayer depends on the endurance of our trust; our determination to cling to God depends on the strength of our trust.' He continues, 'Trust feeds prayer...prayer in return feeds trust – just as the more time I spend with the person I love the deeper grows my connection to him or her.'[civ]

10. After the storm

Yay! You made it. You crossed the lake. You survived the storm – albeit with a few bumps and bruises. But you got there.

And... relax...

No, no chance... there'll be another one along in a minute.

Life's like that, isn't it? We survive one experience and along comes another one. It may be different. It may last longer or shorter. It may be stronger or weaker. But the fact is we move from one experience to another. Sometimes several things happen at once. If it's not one thing it's another thing – and if it's not the other thing, it's both...

So if that's the case, what on earth (or in heaven) was this book all about? 'You've helped me find some stability in times of change,' you might say, 'And now you tell me life isn't going to be stable and it'll all continue to change...'

Fair comment. But let's go back to the lake for a moment. This time on the other side. The western side. The land of Gerasenes. Let's look at what happens to Jesus and the disciples when they step ashore. They've survived one storm and now there's another one – a storm of a totally different nature.

There's a man who's 'Mad, bad and dangerous to know'cv... and there's no time for a risk assessment:

> (Jesus and the disciples) came to the other side of the lake, to the country of the Gerasenes. 2 When Jesus had stepped out of the boat, immediately a man out of the tombs with an unclean spirit met him. 3 He lived among the tombs; and no one could restrain him anymore, even with a chain; 4 for he had often been restrained with shackles and chains, but the chains he wrenched apart, and the shackles he broke in pieces; and no one had the strength to subdue him. 5 Night and day among the tombs and on the mountains he was always howling and bruising himself with stones. 6 When he saw Jesus from a distance, he ran and bowed down before him; 7 and he shouted at the top of his voice, 'What have you to do with me, Jesus, Son of the Most High God? I adjure you by God, do not torment me.' 8 For he had said to him, 'Come out of the man, you unclean spirit!' 9 Then Jesus asked him, 'What is your name?' He replied, 'My name is Legion; for we are many.... (Mark 5:2-9)

This man was somebody's son. He'd been a child who sat on his mother's knee. A boy who splashed in the waters on the western shores of Lake Galilee. And now look at him. He didn't live with the living: he lived with the dead. Whatever happened? Whatever went wrong? The anonymous outcast becomes known by the name of that which possessed him: Legion. He's named by his situation, not the person who he is.

So used was he to being badly treated by other people that when he sees Jesus coming towards him, he is frightened: 'What have you to do with me... do not torment me.' Yet, in his running towards and bowing down before the Lord, he grasped the opportunity to get the help he knew he needed. Like so many people before and since he reached out to Jesus – even though he was afraid of doing so.

Just like with the disciples in the storm, Jesus deals with the fears of this man. Yes, it's a pity about the pigs but Jesus uses that same power to calm the storm that is the life of this man from the country of the Gerasenes. Even then, as the passage goes on to tell us, the 'storm' continued as the crowd hounded Jesus back in to the boat (and who knows, perhaps to face another storm on the lake).

Jesus travelled from one storm into another. A different type, a different strength. Just like us.

Setting sail once more

So, let's sit on the edge of the lake again.

'Do I get in the boat? What if there's a storm? Umm... maybe I'll wait for a calmer day...'

Our previous difficult experiences can make us feel hesitant about turning to face strange but as Vivian Greene wrote: 'Life isn't about waiting for the storm to pass. It's about learning to dance in the rain.'[cvi]

Like it or not, for most of us, a calmer day is not coming. There will always be storms – maybe not always disruptive or damaging but they will happen. Yes, there will also be quieter periods: the storms will pass and calmness can be enjoyed at times too.

The key is to be equipped. To pack the right things in the suitcase. To take with us that which we know works. That which we know will help us navigate the storm. To leave behind those things which don't work or we have found not to be as helpful.

Paula Gooder writes, 'Following Jesus involves tearing up your life plan and throwing it to the wind. Following Jesus may change everything about your life, or just some of it; following Jesus summons you to the biggest adventure of your life. It is hard, uncertain, often vague and unformed, and the most satisfying thing you will ever do.'[cvii]

When the disciples set off in the boat across the lake they didn't know a storm was going to blow up. That doesn't mean the decision to sail was wrong. They went in faith, knowing the balance of probability was it would be ok. It was in the end, despite the storm. And they sailed again... and again... and again.

Acknowledgments

In January 2021, my wife, who (unlike her husband) is often prone to outbursts of excitement, came rushing in saying, 'Richard, there's a message on the answerphone from the Dean of Southwark Cathedral! They've been using Life with St Benedict in online Night Prayer and he wants to talk to you about it.'

It's always lovely to learn that something one has done is being helpful to others. And so it was that my conversations with the Dean, The Very Revd Andrew Nunn, led not only to an online discussion with members of the Cathedral congregation about Benedictine spirituality but also to a Zoom-based Quiet Day on the theme 'Finding Stability in Times of Change.'

Andrew has been a regular source of support ever since and I have benefitted from joining the Cathedral community for online Night Prayer every Sunday evening. I am very grateful to him for writing the Foreword to this book and his generous and kind words.

Those Quiet Days have been run in a number of places online and in person and have helped shape the content of this book. I am grateful to members of the GoHealth Community, Whirlow Spirituality Centre, St Lawrence's, Biddulph, St James', Exeter, St Luke's, Buckfastleigh and the Haldon Mission Community who have played host to such events.

Thank you to Bev Meldrum at Endulini Publishing who recognised the potential for this book and for enabling it to be in your hands. Endulini (isiXhosa language for 'On the Hill') is a brand new, traditional publishing house and I am delighted that this book is their very first one.

And my thanks to Jane, Jon, and Rachel for their love and support over many years of fellow travelling – and to you for reading that which you now hold.

About the author

Richard Frost spent most of his paid employment career helping people to find or remain in work. He specialised in helping those who had a disability or other health conditions and in particular people who experienced depression, anxiety and mental ill health. He was appointed MBE for services to mental health in the Queen's Birthday Honours List in 2018.

He is a licensed lay minister in the Church of England and the author of Life with St Benedict (BRF 2019) which offers daily reflections for modern-day living based on the Rule of St Benedict. A lay member of a Benedictine Monastic Community in England, he is also a chaplain to the South West Ministry Training Course.

Richard writes a blog at www.workrestpray.com and is the author of www.astorytotell.org.uk which considers what we can learn from people who met Jesus. The latter is also available as a book.

His debut novel, Looking to Move On (Chronos Publishing 2022) is a contemporary story of loss and love, the title reflects the message of the book which is one of hope over adversity and that moving on, and rebuilding life, is always possible.

Married to Jane, who is a vicar, they live in Devon, have two adult children and a dog called Daisy.

www.richardfrostauthor.com

Staying Afloat

The sculpture on the front cover is called 'Staying Afloat' by Sarah Ward. Made of plaster, wood and fishing floats, it was part of a special exhibition at The Holburne Museum in Bath in April 2022 entitled 'People Make Museums'. The exhibition was a celebration of creativity and the importance of people in museums and I am grateful to Sarah for permission to use the image.

Sarah writes: 'As we sail through the adventure of life it is rarely clear sailing. In the real world the museum, like a boat, offers a safe space that protects us from the waves when we find ourselves in unchartered waters.

'On board we have a chance to pause, be curious and survey where we have been and where we are going; the past and the future.

'My boats are part of a fleet. Each one is individual but together they sail as a team... so that we can sail together for a while and make connections.

'The sculpture reminds me of calm, happy childhood memories of being with my family by the sea before rough waters hit.

Request for Reviews

Please consider reviewing this book to help us spread the word.

If you enjoyed this book we would be very grateful if you could write a review on the website you purchased it on, for example on Amazon, or on Good Reads.

Alternatively, you can send a review to
endulinipublishing@gmail.com

If you would like to find out about more book releases from Richard Frost and other authors, or you have an idea for a book, check our website and social media pages.

A big thank you from the team at Endulini Publishing.

www.endulinipublishing.com

Notes

[i] David Bowie Changes. Tintoretto Music/RZO Music Ltd, EMI Music Publishing Ltd, Chrysalis Music Ltd 1971

[ii] Coping with Change – author unknown. Original leaflet provided to the author by Church of England Diocese of Exeter

[iii] Coping with Change ibid

[iv] Mark Bradford Seasons of disruption https://www.brf.org.uk/seasons-of-disruption/ 25 April 2021

[v] Bob Dylan The times they are a-changin' © 1963, 1964 by Warner Bros. Inc.; renewed 1991, 1992 by Special Rider Music

[vi] Taken from Jesus 2000 Lion Publishing 1989 pp82-4

[vii] Richard Frost Life with St Benedict BRF 2019

[viii] Richard Frost ibid p11

[ix] Boris Johnson Prime Minister's statement on coronavirus (COVID-19): 23 March 2020 https://www.gov.uk/government/speeches/pm-address-to-the-nation-on-coronavirus-23-march-2020

[x] Met Office https://www.metoffice.gov.uk/weather/guides/coast-and-sea/beaufort-scale

[xi] *Mind Tools The Holmes and Rahe Stress Scale*
https://www.mindtools.com/pages/article/newTCS_82.htm
[xii] *Mind Tools ibid*
[xiii] *Mark Bradford The Space Between BRF 2021 p115*
[xiv] *Sheri Jacobson Avoidance Coping – Is It Adding to Your Anxiety or Depression?*
https://www.harleytherapy.co.uk/counselling/avoidance-coping-depression.htm 18 May 2017
[xv] *Mind Tools https://www.mindtools.com/pages/article/coping-with-change.htm*
[xvi] *Jeremy Sherman Face-it Versus Escapist Coping Strategies in Psychology Today 10 April 2017*
https://www.psychologytoday.com/gb/blog/ambigamy/201704/face-it-versus-escapist-coping-strategies
[xvii] *Kathleen Smith The Psychology Of Dealing With Change: How to Become Resilient https://www.psycom.net/dealing-with-change*
[xviii] *Thomas Merton, The Seven Storey Mountain*
https://twitter.com/monknunCofE/status/1390262890486243329 6 May 2021
[xix] *Quoted by David Adam in Complete Common Worship Sermon Illustrations Kevin Mayhew 2005, 2001 p217*
[xx] *John Drane Introducing the New Testament Lion Publishing 1986 p146*
[xxi] *Martin Turner, Notes from a talk given at Methodist Central Hall, London Feb 2006*
[xxii] *Ray Vander Laan et al, That the World may know*
https://www.thattheworldmayknow.com/sea-of-galilee-

geography

[xxiii] *Efrain Agosto in Feasting on the Word Year B Vol 3 Edited by David L Bartlett & Barbara Brown Taylor Westminster John Knox Press 2009 p167, 169*

[xxiv] *Mark D W Edington in Feasting on the Word Year B Vol 3 Edited by David L Bartlett & Barbara Brown Taylor Westminster John Knox Press 2009 p164*

[xxv] *Mark Bradford The Space Between BRF 2021 p116*

[xxvi] *R. Alan Cole Mark Tyndale New Testament Commentaries IVP 1989 pp154-5*

[xxvii] *Beverly Zink-Sawyer in Feasting on the Word Year B Vol 3 Edited by David L Bartlett & Barbara Brown Taylor Westminster John Knox Press 2009 p167*

[xxviii] *Rudyard Kipling, from 'If' first published in Rewards and Fairies (1910)*

[xxix] *Paul Simon The Boxer Pattern Music Ltd, CBS 1969*

[xxx] *Leon Morris Luke Tyndale New Testament Commentaries IVP 1988 p169*

[xxxi] *Paula Gooder Let me go there Canterbury Press 2016 p95*

[xxxii] *Mark Bradford The Space Between ibid p122*

[xxxiii] *Frank Skinner A Comedian's Prayer Book Hodder & Stoughton 2021 p105*

[xxxiv] *Beverly Zink-Sawyer ibid p169*

[xxxv] *Michael L Lindvall in Feasting on the Word Year B Vol 3 ibid p166*

[xxxvi] *Authorized (King James) Version reproduced by permission of Cambridge University Press, the Crown's patentee in the UK.*

[xxxvii] *Emmaus Road Ministries*

https://emmausroadministries.international/2019/11/24/0-ye-of-little-faith-2/

xxxviii *Efrain Agosto ibid p169*

xxxix *John Bishop Faith Stanford Encyclopaedia of Philosophy https://plato.stanford.edu/entries/faith/ 30 March 2016*

xl *Rachel Frost writing in monthly newsletter St Luke's Bath July 2018*

xli *Greek for 'the Jews' although sometimes used with a negative bias to describe those who opposed Jesus.*

xlii *Eli Lizorkin-Eyzenberg Who Was Nicodemus? https://blog.israelBiblicalstudies.com/jewish-studies/john-3-1-8-who-was-nicodemus-2/ 2013*

xliii *Laurence Cantwell The Quest for the Historical Nicodemus Religious Studies vol 16 No 4 p464 Cambridge University Press 1980 https://www.jstor.org/stable/20005694*

xliv *From Sarum College: http://www.sarum.ac.uk/learning/christian-spirituality/sarum-certificate-in-spiritual-direction*

xlv *Martin G Collins The Miracles of Jesus Christ: Resurrecting Jairus' Daughter https://www.cgg.org/index.cfm/fuseaction/Library.sr/CT/BS/k/1491/Miracles-Jesus-Christ-Resurrecting-Jarius-Daughter.htm 2010*

xlvi *Merriam-Webster Dictionary https://www.merriam-webster.com/dictionary/doubting%20Thomas*

xlvii *Collins Dictionary https://www.collinsdictionary.com/dictionary/english/doubting-thomas*

xlviii *David Adam Complete Common Worship Sermon Illustrations ibid p63*

xlix *Serene Jones in Feasting on the Word - Year B Volume 2 Westminster John Knox Press 2008, 2013 p400*

l *David Stone preaching at Coventry Cathedral 1 May 2011 http://www.coventrycathedral.org.uk/wpsite/wp-downloads/Sermons%20and%20talks/2011-05-01-1030%20-%20Thomas%20-%20John%2020.19-31%20%5BDavid%20Stone%5D.pdf*

li *Jennifer Brown Doubting Thomas – a role model for Christians and scientists https://www.sciencemissioner.org.uk/doubting-thomas-role-model-christians-scientists/ 26 April 2017*

lii *The Contented Life: Spirituality and the Gift of Years by Robert Atwell is published by Canterbury Press*

liii *G Campbell Morgan Why did Jesus go to the temple at 12 years of age? In Christianity https://www.christianity.com/jesus/life-of-jesus/youth-and-baptism/why-did-jesus-go-to-the-temple-at-12-years-of-age.html 13 October 2010*

liv *Nadia Bolz-Weber, author's notes of a talk given at Festival of Preaching, Oxford, 2017.*

lv *Pope Francis speaking at Holy Mass for Families https://w2.vatican.va/content/francesco/en/homilies/2015/documents/papa-francesco_20151227_omelia-santa-famiglia.html 2015*

lvi *There are a number of translations of the Gospel of Philip – for example, by Vladimir Antonov https://holybooks-lichtenbergpress.netdna-ssl.com/wp-content/uploads/The-Gospel-of-Philip.pdf (verse 55) or by Welsey W. Isenburg and the*

Patterson Brown translation at
http://Gospelofthomas.nazirene.org/philip.htm (verse 59)

[lvii] Cally Hammond Augustine's life of prayer, learning and love
BRF 2019 p56

[lviii] Personal communication to author

[lix] Luigi Gioia Say it to God Bloomsbury 2017 p29

[lx] Much of this particular section is taken from Coping after a
traumatic event Royal College of Psychiatrists
https://www.rcpsych.ac.uk/mental-health/problems-
disorders/coping-after-a-traumatic-event

[lxi]

[lxii] https://www.nhs.uk/mental-health/conditions/post-traumatic-
stress-disorder-ptsd/overview/

[lxiii] https://www.nhs.uk/

[lxiv] Such as Mind or Rethink Mental Illness

[lxv] Will Van Der Hart Mental health: the state we're in in Preach
magazine Issue 16 2018 p15

[lxvi] Jo Swinney The Word on Depression in Preach magazine ibid
p26

[lxvii] CBT is a talking therapy and available free through most GP
practices. More information at https://www.nhs.uk/mental-
health/talking-therapies-medicine-treatments/talking-therapies-
and-counselling/cognitive-behavioural-therapy-cbt/overview/

[lxviii] David Adam Complete Common Worship Sermon Illustrations
Kevin Mayhew 2005,2011 p 217

[lxix] Alice Broadway https://twitter.com/alicecrumbs

[lxx] Although often attributed to Maslow, others have been
accredited with its origin. See

https://en.wikipedia.org/wiki/Four_stages_of_competence

[lxxi] Will Van Der Hart ibid p17

[lxxii] Mark Bradford The Space Between ibid p123

[lxxiii] Beverly Zink-Sawyer ibid p169

[lxxiv] Christopher Jamison Finding Sanctuary Weidenfeld &
Nicholson 2006 p53

[lxxv] Cally Hammond ibid p128

[lxxvi] Anonymous The Cloud of Unknowing. There are various
versions of this publication available in print and online.

[lxxvii] Christopher Jamison ibid p61

[lxxviii] Larry Warner Discovering the spiritual exercises of Saint
Ignatius BRF 2020 p104

[lxxix] Beth LaNeel Tanner. Source unknown.

[lxxx] Frank Skinner ibid p11

[lxxxi] There are a number of different translations of the Rule of St
Benedict. One of the most popular is that edited by Timothy Fry
OSB The Liturgical Press 1982. Daily readings of the Rule together
with a reflection can also be found in Life with St Benedict by
Richard Frost BRF 2019

[lxxxii] Joan Chittister OSB, The Rule of Benedict (Crossroad
Publishing, 1992), p60

[lxxxiii] Pope Francis The obedience that sets us free
http://www.vatican.va/content/francesco/en/cotidie/2013/docu
ments/papa-francesco-cotidie_20130411_obedience.html 11 April
2013

[lxxxiv] From the first line of the Prologue of the Rule of St Benedict

[lxxxv] Exact source unknown

[lxxxvi] Quoted by Robert Sarah at

https://www.thecatholicthing.org/2017/07/07/silence-gods-first-language/ 7 July 2007

[lxxxvii] Barbara Brown Taylor, When God is Silent (Canterbury Press, 1998, 2013) p118, 121

[lxxxviii] John Greenleaf Whittier in the hymn, Dear Lord and Father of mankind

[lxxxix] Amy Scott-Robinson Image of the Invisible BRF 2019

[xc] David Walker You are mine BRF 2019 p75

[xci] Frank Skinner ibid p 88

[xcii] Brother Lawrence, The Practice of the Presence of God Mockingbird Classics Publishing, 2015 p55

[xciii] Thomas Merton quoted in notes by Penny Warren for a talk on Desert Spirituality January 2020

[xciv] Cally Hammond ibid p104

[xcv] John Cassian Conferences of John Cassian Conference 9 Chapter 36 Christian Classics Ethereal Library p316

[xcvi] Tim Barnett What We Need to Learn about Prayer from the Early Church
https://www.str.org/w/what-we-need-to-learn-about-prayer-from-the-early-church

[xcvii] Mark Bradford ibid p159

[xcviii] Mark Bradford ibid p124

[xcix] Chris Mason BBC News https://www.bbc.co.uk/news/uk-53602362 31 July 2020

[c] Personal communication to author

[ci] Personal communication to author

[cii] Personal communication to author

[ciii] Steven Croft Comfortable words: a call to restoration BRF 2021

p64

civ *Luigi Giola ibid pp139-40*

cv *A phrase attributed to Lady Caroline Lamb in describing Lord Byron.*

cvi *Vivian Greene http://www.viviangreene.com/*

cvii *Paula Gooder ibid p92*

Printed in Great Britain
by Amazon

11495616R00088